T0065409

Loving
Your Work
Ever After

LOVING YOUR WORK EVER AFTER

A Spiritual Guide to Career Choice and Change

Phyllis M. Taufen
and
Marianne T. Wilkinson

IMAGE BOOKS

Doubleday

New York   London   Toronto   Sydney   Auckland

An Image Book
PUBLISHED BY DOUBLEDAY
a division of Bantam Doubleday Dell Publishing Group, Inc
666 Fifth Avenue, New York, New York 10103

IMAGE, DOUBLEDAY, and the portrayal of a cross intersecting a circle are
trademarks of Doubleday, a division of Bantam Doubleday Dell Publishing
Group, Inc

Scriptural citations are from *The Jerusalem Bible,*
copyright © 1966 by Darton, Longman and Todd, Ltd and
Doubleday & Company, Inc Used by permission of the publisher

Library of Congress Cataloging-in-Publication Data applied for

ISBN 9780385264433
Copyright © 1990 by Phyllis M Taufen and Marianne T Wilkinson
All Rights Reserved
Printed in the United States of America
April 1990

BOOK DESIGN BY PATRICE FODERO

146721804

To our families
whose unique gifts
reflect God's myriad blessings
and who first taught us
the wonder of each person.

Acknowledgments

As we tie the loose ends of our project together for the many dedicated career planners who will read this book, we look back with gratitude to those whose help and support made *Loving Your Work Ever After* a reality.

We thank the behind-the-scenes people who assisted us along the way: Virginia Killingbeck, Darlene Mitchell, Dr. Leonard Doohan, Linda Riggers, SNJM, Anne McCluskey, SNJM, and the Faculty Services personnel at Gonzaga University. The staff at Doubleday deserves thanks, with special mention of Patricia Kossman and Jeanne Connery for expert editing and direction.

In addition, we recognize the directors of and participants in Gonzaga's CREDO Program. Their sense of the need to blend basic job-search skills with spiritual values affirmed our core idea and gave us the opportunity to refine the process.

As we reworked materials each year, we created and consolidated ideas from reading, teaching, and field-testing. We built on the age-old method of experiencing, reflecting, and synthesizing. *Loving Your Work Ever After* underscores the conviction that God wants each of us to be happy and at peace in our daily work—an acknowledgment often overlooked in a society that preaches "success for success' sake." Personal asssessment, market assessment, and the job search will be meaningful if they lead to that end.

We gratefully acknowledge consultants and critics for helping us fashion our guide to career choice. Likewise, we found reinforcement for ideas from business texts and popular manuals. Of particular note is the work of Courtland Bovee and John Thill, Raymond Lesikar, JoAnne Alter, Richard Bolles, Tom Jackson, and Michael Mulligan. Career placement and counseling materials from Whitman College, Wall Walla, Washington; Green River Community College, Auburn, Washington; and Gonzaga University, Spokane, Washington, prove that quality resources can be near at hand. We found them excellent. Professional support through the years from Kevin Pratt, Director of Gonzaga University's Placement and Career Services Center, deserves special commendation.

We continue to learn as new strategies and research come into the career field. The process is not finished—we hope that our book will contribute to the ongoing development of human potential.

Phyllis M. Taufen
Marianne T. Wilkinson

Spokane, Washington
October 21, 1989

Contents

Foreword

As we recalled the stories of Joe, Beth, Carmelita, and Steve, during the writing of this book, we remembered our own story which began over eight years ago.

It was a cold Sunday afternoon in 1981 and we had just finished one of those two-day workshops busy people squeeze into their weekends. As we took off our coats, we looked at each other.

"That wasn't a bad workshop. But did you learn anything you didn't already know?" one of us asked.

"Come to think of it, no."

And then, almost simultaneously, we said, "Why aren't we doing that? Why are we paying someone else to give a workshop on career planning for our community? We could do it!"

With years of experience as teachers and administrators, we had evaluated many candidates, conducted countless interviews, and selected top résumés. In addition, we had recently completed our own successful job searches. (Our individual stories are hidden within these pages!)

It was a memorable moment—an energizing Spark—on a cold Sunday afternoon. We were off and running—working late nights, wondering what we'd gotten ourselves into, and yet excited about the prospect of helping others in a new way. As Sisters of the Holy Names, our charism calls us to "be educators," to work for the "full development of the human person."

We offered our workshop to Gonzaga University's CREDO Program, to which one hundred women and men come each year for renewal. January 1982 found us with our agenda set, worksheets in hand, and overhead projector ready. Participants were enthusiastic; evaluations were positive.

For the next seven years our workshop grew, companies called when employees needed help in job transitions, and letters came from afar asking for copies of our printed handouts. Two years ago, in 1987, we gathered our data into a booklet called *Ministry in the Marketplace* and continued our ministry—still squeezed into our busy work schedules, one as a college teacher and the other an administrator of a drug treatment center.

But God writes straight with crooked lines! And *Loving Your Work Ever After* is such a good example: an example of not knowing what can be done until it's done, and of finding sufficient energy and skills—and time—when the need is great.

Like Christians throughout the centuries, all of us are responsible for using our talents to the full, whether they number ten, five, or one. Buried talents can't build the Kingdom; talents well used can.

Our contacts over these eight years with hundreds of gifted people have convinced us that God does call us to grow through our work experiences—and gives us all we need to do so. Each person has a significant part to play in the fulfillment of creation!

As *Loving Your Work Ever After* grew from a spark of the Spirit, may you grow in wisdom and grace as you turn its pages.

Phyllis M. Taufen, SNJM
Marianne Therese Wilkinson, SNJM

Introduction

Is this the best of times, or the worst of times? If you're honest, you have to admit it's a little of each. Life has its shadows, true, but daisies still bloom in the spring.

As a Christian, you care deeply about your world: family, friends, work, new demands and lingering problems. You strive for a growing awareness of God's presence in daily affairs. And you seek wisdom and courage to face the challenges such awareness opens before you. Contemporary Christianity, perhaps more boldly than ever before, compels you to seek the Kingdom of God right under your own nose. But how?

A story tells about a judge in one of our western states who had the habit of getting in some prayer time as he walked to work at the courthouse each day. His relationship with the Lord was a simple, confident one—and, apparently, vice versa. One morning, on saying goodbye to God at the courthouse's main entrance as was his usual procedure, the gentleman was startled to hear his Friend inquire, "Can't I come in with you sometime and stay the day at work?" From then on, needless to say, a day in the courtroom was never quite the same for this man of faith.

Many men and women in their private prayer journeys today are hearing some similar message. This invitation to a new perspective applies not only to ordained clergy or lay persons called to ministry in a religious or church-related setting; it applies to good people everywhere, like the judge in our story—young people and old, whose sense of God's presence in their lives cannot stop at the reception desk or the time-card board. For them, an hour's dutiful reverence on Sunday or even set times for prayer throughout the week are not sufficient. They seek a deeper relationship. They seek the richness, the peace of God-centeredness throughout the day, every day, including all their hours at work.

For most people, however, earning a living consumes a major portion of their waking hours through forty or fifty years of adult prime time. Supervising the children's ward, serving customers, or typing reports leaves little time for God.

But doesn't it stand to reason that this work should be satisfying, enriching to the spirit, contributing to the good of others—blessed, in other words, by the peace that God's presence inevitably brings? Whether you work in a business office or a factory, a research hospital or your own gift shop in the local mall, and whether you are a new employee or a veteran in the company, you can and should expect the Kingdom to be there at work with you.

It's a struggle to bring your work life honestly and openly to prayer, as well as your prayer to work. But this continual discernment helps keep chosen values in perspective, priorities in order. It is the forum through which you can learn to identify the stirring—be it a mighty wind or the whisper of a breeze—telling you to look closely at what you're doing with so much of your week.

And when you look closely, is there a sense that *your* "kingdom" and God's Kingdom might go hand in hand?

Is it time for a change? The following pages offer some

processes that can help you build a sensitive awareness both of your own needs and of the way God nudges you in regard to them. Use them prayerfully and peacefully rather than anxiously. Anything good takes time.

PART 1

Do You Want a New Job? Thinking It Through

*The kingdom of God is like a treasure hidden in a field,
which someone has found; he hides it again, goes off happy,
sells everything he owns, and buys the field*

Matthew 13:44

It is safe to say there's no such thing as a permanent job.
Scary? Yes, but maybe exciting, too! Permanent means constant, fixed, lasting, unalterable, poured in concrete—or, as
the ancients said, written in flintstone. And whether you've
lived eighteen years or eighty, whether you're fresh from the
classroom, the kitchen, or a part-time job, you know that
change stalks your every path.

In fact, contemporary culture has made it normal, acceptable, and easily possible for many to change not only
their jobs but even their career fields, and to do so not only
once but two or even more times during their working years.
Mid-life dropouts—or rather change-overs—are as common
today as the youthful dropouts of the sixties. And these
change-overs often bring renewed energy and new challenges. Witness the homemaker turned gourmet caterer and
the teacher turned workshop director—or the home handy-
man now helping customers in the neighborhood hardware
store in his later years. So a change, whether from school,
from the home, or from a long-held job, can be a call to a
fuller and even more productive life.

"But why change?" you ask. "How do I *know* it's a sum-
mons to something better?" Well, sometimes experience and
maturity bring new insights. Looking at your successful
neighbor, you realize that you could do that same job; or
volunteering for the hospital gift shop, you recognize your
"gift" for meeting the public. Maybe a feeling of uneasiness
nags at you from the corner of your day and says, "I've got
more than this job demands. I could run the office with half
the confusion." Or maybe sometimes a hidden dream

emerges and you wonder, "What if I returned to school?" Perhaps the negative circumstances of past years disappear and now you can say, "Maybe . . . ?"

Whatever the catalyst—sensing an urge to change, moving to a new city, graduating from school, discovering an opening across town, or finding a partner for that new yogurt shop—maybe change is just the ticket to a happier, more productive life for you.

Happy? Productive? Both? Yes, both! Work and personal pleasure are made for each other and like to "live happily ever after." It would seem obvious that people know whether or not they are happily employed. Surprisingly, however, many choose to stay in unproductive, even unhealthy work situations without realizing what is happening. They're like the man who kept pounding his head against the wall because it felt so good when he stopped. They fail to ask themselves the fair but demanding question: "Do I really want to stay *where* I am, doing *what* I am doing?"

Have you asked yourself this question? Is it lingering behind the bustle of every day? Does your answer have a tentative "no" in it—things aren't just right, but you're not quite sure? Join the club; join the thousands who ponder this question; and join the thousands who hope to answer it somehow this year.

What's going on in your life that suggests a change? In this section we ask you to examine two nudges—one from God and one from life "as it is." Either or both may be the key to your career change; both come under the name of *stress.* You'll look at stress from its positive side—as the urging of the Spirit to some new step in your personal faith journey, of which work is an integral part. Then you'll look at stress from its negative side—as the pressures that fight for and consume your productive energies.

Do you really want a new job? And if so, what should that job be? With faith in your future, take a deep breath, find a cozy spot, relax, and turn the page.

CHAPTER 1

Nudge Number One— God

It's not really a violent push from behind, à la St. Paul, although it might have hit you quite without warning during a weekend retreat or in the middle of a Sunday sermon. More likely, it came in a gradual, unobtrusive way, slipping in around the edges of your consciousness over a period of time. But the nudge is there.

That questioning feeling hit again when you were walking the dog, loading the dishwasher, or pondering tomorrow's schedule. You felt a subtle dissatisfaction with yourself —even when the work was going well, the boss was in a good mood, and your favorite parking space was there waiting for you. "Something is missing," you mused. "Life must hold more."

The Christian Worker

Basically, it's a question you begin asking yourself about where God is in your daily life. About where your gleaning for daily bread is leading—after the bread has been eaten. For a thoughtful and prayerful person, it's an inevitable confrontation with God about building the Kingdom: "Lord, what would you have me do? How does my work add to the whole of creation? What does it matter?"

For the Christian, it does matter—tremendously. The work that you do, in whatever part of the vineyard at whatever season of the turning year, is God's work—somehow. Or could be.

For the Christian, as for the responsible journalist, it *does* matter how things turn out. The reporter and the analyst know that history is affected by what they choose to say or not say. The contractor knows that his work affects those who buy the house—and the waiter knows that his service makes a difference. Any kind of work—done either apart from or in harmony with the Spirit who speaks through peace—will make a difference in "how things turn out." And to the Christian, the way God wants things to turn out is what life is all about.

Happiness

God wants you to be happy along the way, in all facets of your life. A God who loves would never give talents, skills, potential, dreams, and wishes, only to have most of them stifled. A loving God doesn't want pieces of creation to be out of whack—never quite fitting, always in a bind. Depression, undue fatigue, tension, burn-out are not the makings of a peaceful creation. And feeling not quite whole, having hunches about your potential, suspecting that there might be "more"—all these things echo a yearning deep within yourself. Square pegs in round holes never bring peace. Work, however challenging and tiring it is, should help build the Kingdom. And generous sprinkles of joy and enthusiasm, hearty smiles, a sense of a job well done are meant to be part of it all.

So the search goes on for that right place to use your gifts and your experience, to bring your unique presence to bear on a clumsy and faltering world. For you, it's more than a job; it's an act of faith in the person you are and the mission to which you're called. It's acknowledging that your voice in a committee meeting and your willingness to help sell hot dogs at the neighborhood Fun Run are part of the Kingdom's wide and varied mosaic. It's a recognition that you trust God to proclaim the Good News through your daily work in the name of the Creator, the Son, and the Holy Spirit.

God nudges you to love your gifts and enjoy your talents, and to use them where you'll not only do *the job*—whatever and wherever it is—but do it with energy and zest, with peace, patience, and all those other gifts only the Spirit can bring.

Though you recognize the call—from the world around you, from the well deep within—you hesitate. Don't we all? Who wants to risk stepping over the edge, falling flat, or winding up too far from the finish line? But the nudge keeps nudging!

How Do You Know?

How do you know what God asks of you? How do you take the risks inherent in any employment change, whether shifting to a new department or starting a new graduate degree program at the age of forty-five? Wouldn't God be just as well served if you stayed where you are?

If you really believed that, you wouldn't be reading this

book. Uncomfortable a notion as it may be, *you do make a difference.* Gandhi said, speaking from the forum of the heart of God, "Almost everything you do will be insignificant, but it is very important that you do it."

You do it—not your sister or your cousin, not your co-worker or someone "holier." You, with your gifts, your talents, your dreams, and most of all, your peace and joy. The mosaic of life needs your little piece to complete God's creation.

So listen to life's rhythms, disappointments, surprises. Know that God nudges through new technology, soccer games, graduation diplomas, flat tires, and sunsets. Sometimes God points the way through family, a new boss, or an old classmate of ten years ago. Listen. . . . Be ready to be nudged.

WORKSHEET 1

1. What nudges you? Let the Spirit help you jot down your answers to these questions:

    a. Sometimes you wish you could _____

    b. You'd feel better if _____

    c. Now and then you think you'd like to volunteer to _____

    d. If you had time, you'd start _____

    e. If you could change your job, you'd _____

    f. Even if you can't change your job, you'd like to change _____

    g. Your fondest wish is to _____

Go ahead. Ponder now, dream a bit. What if you could change your life, your job, your world? If God stepped into your kitchen for a cup of coffee next Saturday morning, what would you chat about? What would you learn? Have

you chosen "the better part" for your life—or is there something fuller waiting?

If God doesn't actually knock at the back door this week,
might He or She be knocking through those little happen-
ings, serendipities, yearnings, chance encounters, discom-
forts, and successes—all those little pushes, positive and negative—that happen during the week?

WORKSHEET 2

1. What's the positive stress in your life right now? Are you
   being nudged by God? Try these on for size. Check
   those that fit.

   a. _____ Yearning for that "other place/task/sched-
              ule"?
   b. _____ Wishing your work had more meaning?
   c. _____ Dreaming of making a difference in others'
              lives?
   d. _____ Hoping to develop a latent talent?
   e. _____ Having more energy to do more?
   f. _____ Feeling your sense of creativity coming to the
              fore?
   g. _____ Feeling excited about a new challenge?

Reflect quietly upon what positive nudges surface from
the depths of your heart, and write about them.

CHAPTER 2

Nudge Number Two— Life "As It Is"

S Life's Stressors

ometimes the nudge comes from life just "as it is." Stress seeps in through the cracks, and every now and then it takes over the landscape, blanketing every moment of the week. You haven't the luxury to ponder the gentler call of God's nudge to a fuller, richer life. You're too busy facing life as it is.

It's no secret that stress is the most popular root ailment of our day. Its prevalence in the contemporary workplace costs the national economy approximately $150 billion a year in lost productivity, medical benefits, and job-related legal expenses.

Job security—or rather insecurity—in an era of downsizing, technological advances, and corporate take-overs and divestitures, is a haunting demon. Personal values in conflict with market values; changing patterns on the international trade scene; a shifting economic base from industry to service; and the decline of a representative middle class in relation to the growing army of working poor: all of these factors bring into focus the fragile base on which you, the average American worker, now stand. The litany is long but there *is* life beyond the obvious.

Not "Just a Job"

To have a job at all is value enough for some. The comfort of being able to explore the job market, weigh one's own personal skills and values, and prayerfully discern God's will while seeking employment is, for many, a luxury. Or so it seems.

But it is important to realize that having "just a job" or taking "any old job" may multiply the stress factors of your life beyond endurance. Also important is seeing your work situation in a larger framework, seeing that more freedom does exist, that changes can be positive within the problems of the working world.

Roberta's Story

The following true story of a successful school administrator makes the point. Known for her leadership, creativity, and dedication, Roberta built morale, designed a new curriculum, organized parent groups, and kept petunias blooming along the school walkways. But stress crept in, slowly, silently, year after year. Teachers, students, crises walked into her weekends, haunted her nights, and challenged too many of her waking hours. Finally, one rainy day while talking with a colleague, she whispered, "I hate my job. I hate every day. It's the first time in my life that I don't like what I'm doing. But there's nothing else I can do. . . ." The words were out—words she'd never let herself say before—and it seemed to her then that her whole life had crumbled. Stress had brought her to the breaking point because she thought there was noplace else to go. But today she has the freedom of a new job—writing and implementing training programs for corporations—using all the skills and talents she had thought only "fit" one job. Life "as it was" gave way to a wonderful new life "as it is" today.

Facing the Facts

As an individual, become attuned to the stress in your circumstances—recognize it, accept it as such, weigh it in the balance of your personal resources and total life values—and then act. The more you struggle against stress factors, the more energy you expend negatively, and the greater demands you place upon yourself. Balloons can be stretched only so far, personal needs can be stomped on only so long, talents can be buried only so deep!

Frank's Story

Frank worked for a leading bank as marketing director, and did a good job, or so they said. He really didn't know. His carefully crafted letters were signed by the bank's president and went flying across the country to customers and to other corporate headquarters. His brochures, colorful and creative, lay on branch bank counters for clients to pick up and take home. His new seminars for senior citizens proved highly successful. Frank did know, however, that his supervisor cut him out of planning sessions, ridiculed his plans at staff meetings, and watched for the tiniest mistakes on his submitted samples. "Part of the job," he thought, year after year. And the more he produced—he initiated an in-house newsletter and sought departments and individuals to headline in its pages each month, and he gave stiff competition to competitors with his ongoing marketing tools—the more Supervisor Legree demanded. His health problems increased, his workload mounted; and finally, foreseeing no change in supervisors or expectations, Frank risked starting his own marketing business out of his home. And the Cinderella ending of this true story shows him still too busy—but too happy to think about it.

Stressors faced—even when the facing is difficult, as in Frank's case—are stressors defused, if not wholly dismantled. The power of Alcoholics Anonymous. is nowhere clearer than in its simple prayer: "God grant me the serenity to accept the things I cannot change, the courage to change the things I can, and the wisdom to know the difference."

So let's look at the stress in your life. First in your job, and then in related areas. **Thinking it through, do you really want a new job?**

D External Job Stressors

Dissatisfaction with your job, a gnawing feeling of unrest about it, may come from your job itself, either externally or internally. External job stressors include the following:

- an uncomfortable or unsafe physical environment
- difficult working relationships with supervisors and co-workers
- unclear or unreasonable goals
- inappropriate or unjust compensation
- poor management, supervision, policies, and/or procedures

For example, do you have to crawl over others to find the file cabinet? Do you freeze all winter and melt in July? Does your boss get the credit for your outstanding work? Does "walking the extra mile" at your place mean putting in overtime with a smile and receiving no recognition? When you save a situation does the supervisor get the raise? The word "stress" is too gentle for such conditions.

Internal Job Stressors

Internal stressors such as the following are more subtle but can be equally, if not more, debilitating:

- a sense of inadequacy in the skills required for the job
- a sense of "dead end" in career or task options
- a feeling of nonimportance, nonappreciation, non-contribution
- guilt about the quantity or quality of work
- fear of failure or of others' response to one's job performance

Are you, therefore, frantically trying to meet deadlines and feeling frustrated? Do you sense that your job is going nowhere—or in circles? Do you know that the promises made to clients aren't kept or that the guarantees aren't real? Is there a feeling that someone else is creeping into your domain, ready to take over? These are those hard-to-name stressors that lurk just below your consciousness while they take their bites out of your energy and success and happiness.

WORKSHEET 3

1. What *external* stressors from your own work situation come to mind when you re-read the previous list of such stressors?

a. _____

b. _____

c. _____

2. What *internal* stressors of your own jump out when you scan the second list?

a. _____

b. _____

c. _____

Keep these job-related factors in mind as you continue to search out the stressors that might be telling you that a change is in order.

Symptoms of Stress

Before you look deeper, however, check to see if you have any physical symptoms of being stressed. Some signs are clearly evident; many are more complex and may be hidden or disguised. Recognizing your stress signals will help you face them and creatively deal with them.

WORKSHEET 4

1. Here are some common and externally notable signs of stress. Check any that you recognize in yourself.

Past Year			When First Noticed
_____	1.	Persistent fatigue	_____
_____	2.	Tension headache	_____

_____   3. Irritability, grouchiness   _____
_____   4. Restless sleep, insomnia   _____
_____   5. Increased use of alcohol,
             caffeine, relaxants   _____
_____   6. Absenteeism, minor
             illnesses   _____
_____   7. Recurrent infections, virus
             attacks   _____
_____   8. Increased blood pressure   _____
_____   9. Difficulty with emotional
             control   _____
_____   10. Unplanned weight gain or
             loss   _____
_____   11. Nervous habits: e.g., nail
             biting, hair pulling,
             finger drumming   _____
_____   12. Digestive problems   _____
_____   13. Skin eruptions, rashes   _____
_____   14. Dietary cravings   _____
_____   15. Recurring periods of minor
             depression   _____
_____   16. Slowdown in productivity   _____
_____   17. Retreat from personal
             interests   _____

2. Do you find three or more checks in the first column?
   Now look at the duration of the physical symptoms;
   how long have they been present? How long is "too
   long"? Are you asking yourself the question we asked at
   the start of this chapter: Do you want a new job?

   Before deciding that you are in the wrong work situation, however, you may need to look more closely at

the parts as well as the whole. In other words, before you begin the battle, define your dragons.

M Pivotal Sources of Stress

Moving deeper into the external and internal stressors, consider some of their pivotal sources. Get out your pencil again and run down this list.

WORKSHEET 5

Supervision/Authority

1. Who's actually the boss? _____

2. Who *thinks* he or she is the boss? _____

3. Who tells you what to do? _____

4. Is he or she a) okay? b) considerate? c) an ogre?
   d) other _____

5. Whom do you tell what to do? _____

6. Is this "telling" a) easy? b) hard? c) enjoyable?
   d) impossible? _____

7. Who gets the credit for your job well done? _____

8. Why? _____

Attitudes/Co-worker Relationships

1. What's the prevailing atmosphere at work? (One
   word only.) _____

2. Who makes it that way? _____

3. Who builds morale? _____

4. How? _____

5. Who lowers morale? _____

6. How? _____

7. Who do you wish would leave? _____

8. Stay? _____

Physical Environment

1. What three things do you like as is? _____

2. What would you change? _____

3. Why? _____

4. What *can* you change? _____

5. Why don't you? _____

6. What can't you change? _____

7. Why can't you? _____

Schedule/Time Issues

1. What's right with your schedule? _____

2. What's wrong? _____

3. Why? _____

4. How would you change it? _____

5. Can you? _____

Salaries/Benefits

1. Does your salary accurately reflect the work done? _____

2. What would be commensurate? _____

3. What benefits do you have? _____

4. What should you have? _____

5. Can you do anything about salary/benefits? _____

6. How? _____

Materials/Equipment/Support

1. What do you need that you don't have?

    materials: _____

    equipment: _____

    support: _____

2. What do you have that you don't need? _____

3. What can you do about the situation? _____

Rules/Regulations

1. Which ones help your work? _____

2. Which hinder it? _____

3. Who makes the rules and regulations? _____

4. Do you have any power to change them? _____

5. How? _____

Job Security

1. How secure are you in your job? Circle one:
    expendable   insecure   either/or   secure
    indispensable

2. How do you know? _____

3. If not sure, how can you find out? _____

4. What would change your degree of security? _____

5. Is that feasible now? _____

Ethical/Moral Issues

1. Can you accept the ethics of your job situation?

   _____

2. Can you live out your values of honesty, integrity, etc.? _____

3. What conflicts with your moral values? _____

4. What can you do to change the environment? _____

How's that for looking at life "as it is"? Take a break now and do your favorite leisure activity. Like computers that display the signal "Please Wait" at the bottom of their screens, your brain probably just sent the same signal to you!

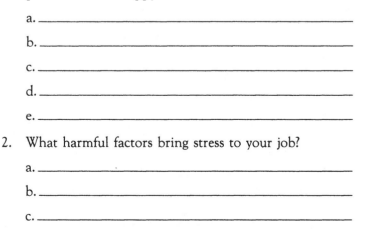

Positive/Negative Factors

WORKSHEET 6

1. Now gather up the "goodies" and list the positive factors from the preceding list that make your work both productive and happy:

   a. _____

   b. _____

   c. _____

   d. _____

   e. _____

2. What harmful factors bring stress to your job?

   a. _____

   b. _____

   c. _____

d. _____

e. _____

3. Is the picture becoming clearer? Which is winning—the positive or the negative side?

Coming Full Circle

Coming full circle after examining the parts, let's look again at the big picture. Maybe you're in the "land of make-believe." Maybe what you *say* your job is—isn't what *it is*.

Job Description

Job description! If you don't have one, no wonder you're feeling uncomfortable. Are your responsibilities and tasks at the present time actually the same as those described in your original job description? Or have other "little" duties and chores become part of your routine without your knowing it? Check it out.

WORKSHEET 7

Main Duties in Job Description	What You Actually Do
1. _____	_____
2. _____	_____
3. _____	_____
4. _____	_____
5. _____	_____

How do the two lists compare? Tuck this information into your decision-making process and let it point out some causes for stress.

Evaluation Facts

Check your evaluation program, growth-assessment charts, or whatever is used to measure your efficiency and worth to the establishment. If you don't have one, how do you know the quality of your work, the strong points that make you stand out in performance? How do you know the weaknesses that need to be worked on? How can you win if you don't know the requirements of the game?

WORKSHEET 8

1. If you do have regular assessment sheets or evaluative tools, take a look at your most recent one.

My Last Evaluation:

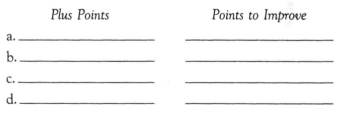

Plus Points	*Points to Improve*
a. _____	_____
b. _____	_____
c. _____	_____
d. _____	_____

2. Does stress prowl around these facts?

Other Life Stressors

To be completely open about stress on the job, it's necessary to also look at the rest of your life just as carefully. Use the following worksheet to review current stress factors arising in areas of your life that are not job-related.

Perhaps help from that close friend, whose common sense and love for you are strong, can be invaluable. Sometimes, through a sense of duty, guilt, or pride, you may prefer not to name certain situations, persons, or conditions that are true stressors. But unless they are acknowledged, they will continue to be powerful forces undermining your work and your happiness. To name is not to condemn or reject; it is to come to terms with.

WORKSHEET 9

1. Look at these facets of your life as it is today and see what's good and what's stressful in it.

Family/Marriage

You're glad about: *You'd like to change:*

a. _____   _____

b. _____   _____

c. _____   _____

Neighborhood/Community

It's good that: *You wish that:*

a. _____   _____

b. _____   _____

c. _____   _____

Church

You like: *You'd prefer:*

a. _____   _____

b. _____   _____

c. _____   _____

Friends/Relationships

Good points are: *Need improvement:*

a. _____   _____

b. _____   _____

c. _____   _____

Personal Issues

You're glad about: *You really dislike:*

a. _____   _____

b. _____   _____

c. _____   _____

Spirituality/Prayer

Your strengths are: *You need to improve in:*

a. _____   _____

b. _____   _____

c. _____   _____

Other Areas of Life

You need to look at:

a. _____

b. _____

c. _____

Feeling stressed? Walk around the block, have a cup of tea, grab that tennis racket and pound a few balls against the side wall, or go mow the lawn. Come back refreshed and ready to summarize a few more facts.

Who's to Blame:
Clare's Story

Who or what is really responsible for your stress? The following story might help you to answer this question. Clare was a competent secretary—the kind every administrator dreams of "owning." And "owned," Doctor X did. Reports were typed at the last minute and sent flying via Federal Express with the professional touch needed to win the contract. Appointments were carefully made, clients graciously met, and the routine paperwork, no matter how deep, efficiently disposed of. Doctor X thought all went well; Clare smiled and acquiesced with nary a wrinkle in her brow or her composure. At home, however, Clare collapsed and complained. She went to work earlier in the morning, stayed later at night, and often sneaked over to the office on Saturday mornings. She needed a "bit of wine" after work until bedtime, moaned about her job, and recounted the pressures of each day. Headaches were frequent and her blood pressure rose. Family and friends suggested talking with Doctor X about the overload and the need for another secretary —at least part-time. Clare heard nothing. Co-workers suggested that she was being taken advantage of, that she not accept the added duties given to her month after month. Clare heard nothing. For six years she slaved at that job, complaining about her work, the overload, the stress. For six years she did nothing to change the situation and finally had to quit—the job had taken its toll. She was indignant when Doctor X easily hired two secretaries to replace her. She had never realized that she caused much of the stress, having been unable to let go of responsibilities, unable to face the fact of unreasonable work, unable not to be indispensable to Doctor X, whom she had served without question.

WORKSHEET 10

Ask yourself three good questions about the stressors you have named in the preceding worksheet, # 9, and jot down the answers quickly in the following spaces provided for your ideas.

1. Does most of the stress you named come from *something objective* over which you have *little or no control,* or from *your own response or attitude* toward something, an attitude and response *you do control?*

_____

_____

_____

2. Are the stressors related to a responsibility *you are choosing to hold onto* as opposed to one *you could share if you were willing to?*

_____

_____

_____

3. How are the stressors *affecting job performance?*

_____

_____

_____

_____

_____

CHAPTER 3

The Challenge to Act

Keys to Change

After a good look at the factors in your life suggesting a career or job change—whether stemming from God's nudge, life "as it is," or any unique facet of your life—a decision must be made. The time you've already spent **thinking it through—asking yourself if you want a new job**—indicates that no important decision is really made with the fall of a gavel. What really goes into a well-discerned career or job change? Here are some keys.

1. *Ongoing career assessment.* Regular review of your achievements, relationships, and satisfaction is important. Take time to reflect periodically about "how things are going" or to question whether they are "going" at all. Don't let yourself be surprised by a crisis—see it coming over the horizon.

2. *Periodic goal-setting* Think where you'd like to be six months from now, a year, five years. Who's helping

you get there? Who's hindering you? What steps should you take, or avoid? Life's quirks often make the road unknown; but setting goals, even though they may not be achieved, brings more direction to your life than does never setting goals at all.

3. *A support system.* A prayer circle, a cluster of close and prudent friends, a spiritual advisor, a spouse. One person or a small group. Be sure you have listeners in your life. Advisors are a dime a dozen, but listeners are straight from Tiffany's.

4. *An at-homeness with yourself and your gifts.* The activities in Part II will help you achieve this at-homeness. Self-knowledge and self-acceptance are vital in career decision-making. They are your personal guides for the journey. "Where to?" asks first "Who?" and "With what?"

5. *A decision to make a decision.* Whether your decision is to stay in your current situation, move within your field, or completely change your career direction, make a decision and live with it. Review it annually —maybe more often—but in the meantime live with it boldly, both as a matter of principle and as a plus for your career. Half-hearted, poorly committed work brings half-hearted and poorly delivered recommendations when you need them.

Make prayer integral to your career path. As you use these five keys—your present status, goals, support system, giftedness, and decisions—you'll be talking to and with the Lord. That's what prayer is: talking about life with Someone who cares mightily about how your life goes. You probably remember Tevye in *Fiddler on the Roof.* He didn't use very many "Thee"'s and "Thou"'s but told God "like it is" and asked some remarkably hard questions.

Exploring the Risks

Living organisms either move ahead or regress; life and stagnation are incompatible. And in the workplace, some intervals of change are healthy. The more this change is guided by personal integration and deepening spirituality, the healthier it will be.

Although making any work change involves considerable risk, such a shift often releases hidden energy you never knew you possessed. You discover that something "more" that God or life has been nudging you toward.

But how much risk you can handle at any given time is measured by your personal integration, and your ability to trust that God cares and supports how things are going with *you*.

How much risk can you tolerate at this time in your life? The following exercise invites you to look at some factors spelling R-I-S-K for most people.

WORKSHEET 11

Ready for some math? Rate each of the following statements on a scale of 0 to 3:

> 0 = not a consideration for me at all just now
> 1 = somewhat of a consideration right now
> 2 = a high consideration for me
> 3 = impossible even to consider

If you make a (career, job, status) change at this time:

_____ you may alter your compensation plan.

_____ you may alienate or disappoint those you feel loyalty toward.

_____ you may prove unequal to the requirements or expectations of the new situation.

_____ your benefits (pension plan, insurance, vacation, etc.) may change.

_____ you may not have the physical or psychic energy to see the new venture through.

_____ you may diminish or lose prestige and/or recognition that you currently enjoy.

_____ you may not find support from family, friends, others you love and respect.

_____ you may be more successful than you really want to be.

_____ you may have to accept greater responsibility.

_____ you may be confronted with new surroundings, relationships.

_____ negative or false motives may be imputed to your decision to change.

The lower your score, the better the chances that you're ready to move—maybe not quite tomorrow, but in the very near future.

Making the Decision

Some trips are never taken because the traveler continues to plan, read two more brochures, check out alternate routes, and readjust wardrobe articles. So, too, it may be with career change.

Somewhere, however, the pattern of wondering and reflecting must be broken and alternatives judged on their relative merits. Don't follow the example of the new cook who lined up so many recipes and checked so many suggested menus that the guests arrived before the final decisions were made. Peanut butter sandwiches and carrot sticks were nourishing but not what the evening called for.

Use the following process to get your thoughts down on

paper. Then—and only then—move on to the next sections: self-assessment, attitudes, job market, and tools. These pages will affirm your decisions as they are jotted down here—and make them real, the right ones, the blessed ones. Or help you circle back with new insights and courage!

WORKSHEET 12

1. Your alternatives are (check only those truly open to you):

    _____ to remain in your present situation.

    _____ to seek adjustment within your present organization (different job/department/responsibility for the same employer).

    _____ to seek a new job outside of this organization.

    _____ to entirely alter your career direction.

2. For each alternative *identified as open to you,* list the advantages, disadvantages, and risks as you see them:

Alternative   Advantages   Disadvantages   Risks

a. _____

_____

_____

_____

b. _____

_____

_____

_____

c. _____

_____

_____

_____

d. _____

_____

_____

_____

3. Considering all of the advantages, disadvantages, and risks for each alternative, list the alternatives in order from the most desirable to the least.

a. _____

b. _____

c. _____

d. _____

Your top-ranked alternative deserves your full attention now. Take it to prayer and ask the Lord to confirm the decision with you. Be willing to wait for confirmation through the daily unfolding of events. Both God and life "as it is" will let you know what to do. Ask for a listening heart so you will be ready to respond to the decision you've made in faith and trust. Believe firmly that if God has other preferences for you, another alternative will emerge—and with it the courage to accept. Move ahead with confidence.

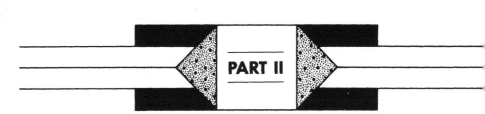

PART II

What Are Your Skills and Values? Self-Assessment

There is a variety of gifts but always the same Spirit; there are all sorts of service to be done, but always to the same Lord; working in all sorts of different ways in different people, it is the same God who is working in them.

I Corinthians 12:4–7

One of the most difficult things for *adult* human beings to accept is their own giftedness. Children, on the other hand, refreshingly delight in demonstrating their abilities, bringing smiles all around with their triumphant and unaffected, "Look—I did it all by myself!"

Why do we lose that spontaneous joy in our own accomplishment, our own achievement, as the years move on? Where does our "clown," our "free spirit" go? Who says we're not good? Why don't we believe the words of the poster that proclaims, "God doesn't make junk!"

Is this the result of cultural conditioning, social convention, old-fashioned "humility"? Whatever it is that makes us re-program ourselves from appreciating our gifts to hiding them in shy diffidence—the die is cast. Sadly, we become self-deprecators; the self-putdown is one of contemporary Western civilization's most uncivilized characteristics.

Although it's obvious that you can't give what you don't have, it's also obvious that before you can market yourself, you must *know* and *accept* your talents and skills. And furthermore, you will have to get in and prove that you know them, by presenting them through the job-search tools: résumé, cover letter, interview, follow-up.

Reversion to childhood? No, call it rather a renewal of the spirit of Eden, that innocence and simplicity of the human person as designed by God. Aren't your gifts, after all, God's? Isn't the development you have drawn out of them over the years *your* faithful response to what was first given in love?

Only when you know your self, your gifts, your skills, can you seek a new job or a career that matches them. This section is designed to help you analyze your talents and then list the skills that come from these talents. When you've seen your long list of skills, you can cluster them into a profile that reflects the real YOU. Finally, after achieving this perspective on yourself and talking it over with the Lord, you'll come to know and love all those talents, skills, and gifts you can take to a new job or career.

As you proceed through the activities of this section, have a good time. You often find your gifts not in the job you're presently doing but in those other activities you choose to do "on the side." These experiences sometimes reveal the you that you've never thought about.

So there's absolutely no excuse for giving minus marks to anything about yourself, if you're being really honest and open. Here's God once again giving you a chance to rejoice in the YOU that you are. As Shakespeare wrote, "What greater praise than this: that you alone are you."

CHAPTER 4

The Visible You: Talents and Skills

A *talent* is a gift, ability, potentiality. A *skill* is an expertise, technique, virtuosity. Talents are inborn; skills are developed. Talents are there—*boom!* Skills come along gradually. One of the world's greatest tragedies is the nondevelopment of human talent. Do you know anybody with a talent that's still buried, waiting to bloom?

There's no doubt that God provides all the talent needed for human beings to make their world—and their lives—beautiful, peaceful, comfortable to live in. Too often, however, these talents are left to wither for want of nurturing, for lack of support, or because there's no one to help hoe the weeds.

But fortunately for all, many talents do have a chance to grow. Many people have developed at least some personal talents over the years, some to a remarkably accomplished degree. Witness the local barber-shop quartet, the sign painter across the street, or the church organist who's been pumping the organ since her feet first reached the pedals! Your talents, too, have been ripening.

Skills Come from Talents

Generally speaking, it's the skills you have—the skills developed through practice, sometimes through trial and error, always over time—that are your market products in the job search. Employers want results. Demonstrate that you have the skills to achieve those results, even better ones than the employer expected, and you probably have the job! And skills often come from talents—talents you've used sometimes without even knowing it.

Find Your Talents First

Use the next worksheet as an exercise in showcasing your personal talents. Ask yourself, and ask others whose opinion you value and trust, what talents—*native gifts*—you possess. Then ask how you—and those chosen others— know this. What do you do that demonstrates your talents? Are you handy around the house? Artistic? Able to console others? A good cook? What do you *like* to do? Here's a chance to review short, short stories from your own life that may give you a chuckle, a blush, or even a warm lump in the throat.

Look at the examples given in this next worksheet and then fill in your own unique gifts or talents.

WORKSHEET 13

List your talents, any proof of your talents and a person or persons who helped you—through encouragement, challenge, or support—to bring each talent to where it is now.

Talent	Proof of Your Talent	Person(s) Who Helped You Develop It Along the Way
Example: Good Cook	People like to eat my dinners—love my apple pies and whole wheat rolls. I'm always asked to help with the church dinner.	Mom showed me how to cook as I was growing up. My Home Ec Teacher, Mrs. Cody, in high school, also taught me.

a. _____

_____

_____

_____

b. _____

_____

_____

_____

c. _____

_____

_____

_____

d. _____

_____

_____

_____

e. _____

_____

_____

_____

If you need more space, go ahead and get another piece of paper and carry on. Don't stop until you've claimed them all!

W Then Look at Your Skills

While doing the previous worksheet, you probably thought about how others know your giftedness. And perhaps, as you pondered alone, you gained some new insights about people you too often take for granted. High-level skills are often developed so matter-of-factly, day in and day out, that we are unaware of the process. One day someone says, "What a marvelous cook you are!" and you suddenly realize, "Well, I guess I have picked up a few tricks." It's more than a few tricks that gets a six-course Thanksgiving dinner to the table in perfect coordination and turns out pie crust even Aunt Cynthia raves about!

T Ella's Story

This true story shows how a talent can blossom into skills needed in the job market. Ella liked to cook, and while raising her family on a limited budget she learned how to make soup—soup that was nourishing *and* delicious. Carrot peelings, celery tops, and potato skins went into the "stock pot" and came out in the form of a rich broth, ready for rice, macaroni, or pearl barley. When her church decided to have simple suppers now and then, Ella volunteered to help. Little by little, Ella's soup—huge cauldrons of it—became famous. Parishioners asked for the recipes; Ella obliged. Then her bread—fresh and scrumptious—became well-known and recipes were again requested. Today, Ella and several other ladies of the church manage a popular little lunch café where—you guessed it—homemade soups and breads top the menu.

Signs that You Have a Skill

It's often the skills you take most for granted that you rely on to see you through. Skills that are transferrable, that make you versatile and thus valuable for the long haul.

The common phenomenon of mid-life career shifts seen throughout the nation at present is evidence of this kind of skill transference. By choice, rather than economic necessity, business executives are opening cabinet shops, blue-collar workers are programming computers, physicians are entering seminaries. After years of work—often very good and productive work—men and women are discovering that they have the basic skills they need to leave one career path for another without undue anxiety. They can pursue what has sometimes been a lifelong dream because they have all they need to do so! And they are renouncing with a clear conscience the tired and thoroughly un-Christian ethic that if something is what you want to do, it must be wrong; that if it hurts, it's good.

How do you know you really have a skill? The following scenario may help to guide you.

1. You have opportunities, or you go out and seek opportunities, to practice what might be a skill.

2. You find satisfaction in practice; more satisfaction as you progress.

3. You receive some reinforcement from your practice: awards, recognition, encouragement from others. As

simple as a sincere, "That's beautiful, Joe" or "May I have your recipe?"

4. You feel confident in sharing what you can do with others.

5. You can look back and see the progress you've made from your first attempts to the present. And you like what you see!

6. You know enough about what you do and how you do it to also know you're not perfect in the skill, and you're willing to keep improving.

Look Deeper

Look deeper into the activities or experiences that you've found rewarding during the past years. Here is where you'll find your talents blossoming into skills you've probably never analyzed. Whether you find new frontiers or familiar homesteads, or a little of both, your remembering will help you deepen your sense of God's gifts to you—gifts that will not be left behind when you enter the office or workshop, but carried with you throughout all the hours of the workday, all the workdays of your life.

What Do You Discover?

Depending on your age, select a representative period of your most recent past. Consider the last twenty years if you're a venerable mid-lifer, ten years if you're younger, even three years if you're fresh out of school. Write the beginning year and the current year on WORKSHEET # 14.

Relax and let the "cream" experiences from those years rise to the surface of your consciousness. What did you do during those years that energized you? Such experiences might have entailed hard work, late hours, difficult challenges, but they were positive. They fit your style!

Take your time. These experiences may or may *not* have been paid jobs or other employment. They could have been such things as working on the senior prom committee, participating in the neighborhood Kiddie Co-Op, or working with Big Brothers and Sisters. But be aware of the things that come to mind first. Jot down as many as you want; make sure you liked doing them! Following is a partial list of the satisfying experiences selected by two individuals.

Peter:

- remodeling the kitchen
- negotiating the Stevens contract
- working with Kiwanis on the soccer field project
- helping with the retirement banquet for the company president
- teaching fly-tying

Paula:

- making Sandy's wedding dress
- getting the neighborhood to sign up for Block Watch
- covering the office when Jim's assistant was on maternity leave
- serving on the church council of elders
- planning the family reunion picnic

Now go ahead with your review, and record the results on the following worksheet. Do not be governed by a sense of what *ought* to have been satisfying, such as your obligations and responsibilities. Perhaps they were positive; perhaps they were not. Be honest in your choices—no one will be checking on you. Listen to your heart!

WORKSHEET 14

1. From 19___ to 19___, you truly enjoyed doing these things:

   a. _____

   b. _____

   c. _____

   d. _____

   e. _____

   f. _____

   g. _____

   h. _____

   i. _____

   j. _____

2. Wasn't it fun to think back on those good times? Now, among all your choices, what *five* experiences stand out for you as the best, the most satisfying of all? When you've made your decision, list your favorite five here:

   a. _____

   b. _____

   c. _____

   d. _____

   e. _____

   Each experience has its own story of the *who*, the *what*, the *when*, and the *why*—along with the jokes, the crises, and the never-to-be-forgotten details. Before you sketch out the stories of your five most enjoyable experiences, take time to read Joe's account of a challenging and, for him, enjoyable experience.

Joe's Story

In 1985, I had the job of directing the choir for the Cathedral centennial celebration. I needed to make the vocal music not only excellent musically, but also integral to the whole centennial program.

As usual, we were pressed for time because the centennial committee was late in deciding final dates and other details; even up to three weeks before the event, we weren't sure who the principal celebrant would be.

I had to work closely with the pastor and three members of the Cathedral staff as well as the liturgy committee of lay people, not to mention the choir organist, maintenance crew, those decorating the church . . . Communications were difficult at best.

Several members of the parish had their noses out of joint because we decided not to sing any Latin. The parish administrator was a tightwad and wouldn't approve any purchases until it was almost too late to get materials for rehearsal. I remember thinking, "If I make it through with these people, I can make it through anything!"

But you know, as I remember, it was the people, too, who made it all fun. So many came through in a pinch with far more than I ever could have expected. For everyone who was difficult to work with, I can recall two who were real gems.

Finally, when I had recruited a good mix of voices, selected the music, gone to all the centennial committee meetings, negotiated for the risers and other staging, and stayed within the budget, along with going through long rehearsals, it was great. People are still talking about the whole affair—and they always mention the choir and the music! I'd do it all again—in a minute. It was really fun!

Your Story

Looking a bit closer, recall each of your five top experiences. Each one has its own story. Details probably flashed before your eyes as you remembered them. Using the following sections for each experience, tell its story.

WORKSHEET 15

Answer these quick questions as you remember the details, the humor, the crises, the challenges, and how much you enjoyed it all—or most of it!

Experience or Job #1:

What was the job? _____

_____

_____

_____

What needed to be done? _____

_____

_____

_____

What were the problems? _____

_____

_____

_____

Who else was involved? _____

_____

_____

_____

What feelings were significant for you? _____

_____

_____

_____

What did you *actually do?* _____

_____

_____

_____

_____

_____

_____

Experience or Job #2:

What was the job? _____

_____

_____

_____

What needed to be done? _____

_____

_____

_____

What were the problems? _____

_____

_____

_____

Who else was involved? _____

_____

_____

_____

What feelings were significant for you? _____

_____

_____

_____

What did you *actually do?* _____

_____

_____

_____

_____

_____

_____

Experience or Job #3:

What was the job? _____

_____

_____

_____

What needed to be done? _____

_____

_____

_____

What were the problems? _____

_____

_____

_____

Who else was involved? _____

_____

_____

_____

What feelings were significant for you? _____

_____

_____

_____

What did you *actually do?* _____

_____
_____
_____
_____
_____
_____

Experience or Job #4:

What was the job? _____

_____
_____

What needed to be done? _____

_____
_____

What were the problems? _____

_____
_____

Who else was involved? _____

_____
_____

What feelings were significant for you? _____

_____
_____

What did you *actually do?* _____

_____

_____

_____

_____

_____

_____

Experience or Job #5:

What was the job? _____

_____

_____

_____

What needed to be done? _____

_____

_____

_____

What were the problems? _____

_____

_____

_____

Who else was involved? _____

_____

_____

_____

What feelings were significant for you? _____

_____

_____

_____

What did you *actually do?* _____

_____

_____

_____

_____

_____

_____

_____

What great experiences you've had. Looking back at them, knowing that you made a difference, seeing how it all fit together in spite of difficulties and setbacks—all this helps the picture of your particular (and marketable!) skill package to take shape.

Finding YOUR Pattern and Place

In this section you will find another worksheet waiting to help put your skills into a pattern, a pattern that will reveal you and your skills—the *you* who's longing to fit into *your* special spot in God's wide and wonderful creation.

Take a peek and see dozens of skills sprinkled on the next pages. Some of them are yours—some are not. But this worksheet will help to reveal the you who might be ready for a new job and a new excitement in life.

WORKSHEET 16

1. Start with *Experience or Job #1* that you listed and analyzed on page 48.

2. Then go slowly through the whole skill list that follows and put a check mark in front of each skill you used in this experience or job under column marked #1. (Be

sure to work through the whole skill list before starting over with Experience or Job #2.)

3. Take your time, be honest, and don't apologize over anything.

4. If you're in doubt about whether you used that skill or not, it may be better to skip it.

Pray about what you are going to do, asking for a simple spirit and an honest memory. Give God permission to surprise you, and promise you'll love the surprise. Because you will.

Now go ahead, and once again check off each skill you used in Experience or Job #1, then #2, and on to Job #5. Have a good time!

Skill Groups

JOB	1	2	3	4	5
A.					
Selling goods, services	—	—	—	—	—
Motivating people	—	—	—	—	—
Promoting causes, products	—	—	—	—	—
Developing markets	—	—	—	—	—
Reconciling differences	—	—	—	—	—
Initiating action	—	—	—	—	—
Public speaking	—	—	—	—	—
Managing volunteers	—	—	—	—	—
Lobbying for action	—	—	—	—	—
Generating confidence	—	—	—	—	—
B.					
Writing (literary)	—	—	—	—	—
Composing music	—	—	—	—	—
Working with crafts	—	—	—	—	—
Working with symbols	—	—	—	—	—
Illustrating	—	—	—	—	—
Drawing, painting	—	—	—	—	—
Designing	—	—	—	—	—

	1	2	3	4	5
Singing, playing musical instrument	—	—	—	—	—
Dancing, choreography	—	—	—	—	—
Directing chorus, instrumental group	—	—	—	—	—
C.					
Supervising others	—	—	—	—	—
Correcting weaknesses in systems, procedures	—	—	—	—	—
Training others	—	—	—	—	—
Interpreting policy, directives	—	—	—	—	—
Identifying channels	—	—	—	—	—
Scheduling	—	—	—	—	—
Setting goals, objectives, standards	—	—	—	—	—
Analyzing information	—	—	—	—	—
Evaluating	—	—	—	—	—
Delegating	—	—	—	—	—

	1	2	3	4	5
D.					
Thinking clearly, logically	—	—	—	—	—
Reporting, reviewing	—	—	—	—	—
Translating	—	—	—	—	—
Editing	—	—	—	—	—
Writing (expository)	—	—	—	—	—
Defining terms	—	—	—	—	—
Proofreading, correcting	—	—	—	—	—
Clear speaking	—	—	—	—	—
Synthesizing information	—	—	—	—	—
Summarizing	—	—	—	—	—
E.					
Advising, explaining	—	—	—	—	—
Affirming, encouraging	—	—	—	—	—
Modifying behavior	—	—	—	—	—
Listening accurately, effectively	—	—	—	—	—
Demonstrating processes, procedures	—	—	—	—	—
Trying different approaches	—	—	—	—	—
Creating examples	—	—	—	—	—
Paraphrasing	—	—	—	—	—

	1	2	3	4	5
Coaching	—	—	—	—	—
Analyzing questions	—	—	—	—	—
F.					
Improvising, adapting	—	—	—	—	—
Integrating diverse elements	—	—	—	—	—
Employing theory	—	—	—	—	—
Using memory, intuition	—	—	—	—	—
Thinking of, applying new ways, materials	—	—	—	—	—
Planning ahead, thinking of the future	—	—	—	—	—
Taking risks	—	—	—	—	—
Using imagination	—	—	—	—	—
Seeing relationships others miss	—	—	—	—	—
Verbalizing new or unusual ideas, solutions	—	—	—	—	—
G.					
Appraising, estimating, assessing	—	—	—	—	—
Maintaining accuracy	—	—	—	—	—
Reading, interpreting detail	—	—	—	—	—

	1	2	3	4	5
Recognizing, appreciating talent and skills					
Pertinent questioning					
Appreciating facts, data					
Working with precision					
Identifying potential					
Observing					
Careful listening					

H.

	1	2	3	4	5
Taking charge in emergencies					
Making difficult decisions					
Starting projects, initiating					
Taking risks					
Persevering in tasks					
Volunteering for difficult tasks					
Making changes					
Taking responsibility					
Working independently					
Responding calmly, quickly to needs, circumstances					

I.

	1	2	3	4	5
Gathering data					
Applying criteria					
Judging objectively					
Ascertaining causes					
Sorting information					
Organizing data					
Working comfortably with detail					
Using logic					
Maintaining careful records					

J.

	1	2	3	4	5
Manipulating materials skillfully					
Working with hands: typing, sewing, etc.					
Fixing mechanical things					
Fitting, assembling					
Cleaning					
Building, constructing					
Repairing equipment, furniture					
Selecting appropriate parts					

	1	2	3	4	5
Analyzing mechanical problems					
Doing close visual work					
K.					
Running, jogging, hiking					
Swimming, water sports					
Navigating, steering, driving equipment					
Gardening, logging, farming					
Team sports					
Working with, training animals					
Fishing, hunting					
Enduring difficult physical conditions					
Picking fruit, harvesting					
Using physical coordination					
L.					
Checking on details, accuracy					
Organizing things, data					
Keeping on schedule					
Handling repetition well					

	1	2	3	4	5
Respecting, using protocol					
Managing resources well: time, money, etc.					
Being discrete					
Attending to little things, loose ends					
Following established procedures					
Keeping good records					
M.					
Acting, directing, producing					
Making presentations to audiences					
Telling stories, holding attention					
Being poised in public situations					
Being sensitive, responsive to others					
Clowning, making people laugh					
Thinking on your feet					
Maintaining control under stress					
Reading aloud					
Generating personal participation from others					

	1	2	3	4	5
N.					
Nursing, helping physically					
Being tactful, gentle					
Showing interest in, concern for others					
Interacting easily with new people					
Caring for multiple needs of people					
Facilitating personal relationships					
Working well with a team					
Managing hospitality					
Listening actively					

	1	2	3	4	5
O.					
Analyzing number information					
Estimating costs, trends					
Banking					
Administering financial resources					
Negotiating financial matters					
Working with statistics					
Doing inventory					
Keeping accurate records, reports					
Budgeting					
Computing, calculating, monitoring numbers					

Gaining Perspective

Great work! Did you enjoy basking in the good times, recalling how you helped things turn out the way they did? Can you see a bit more clearly in retrospect how God can write straight with crooked lines?

Throughout your work life, God has been molding, honing, polishing you through the opportunities set before you. You've been a partner in a process that has unimaginably significant results, not only for you but for countless others you may never know.

You've probably also discovered that your skills cluster in one or more skill groups—and this is fine. Skills build on one another, relate to one another in a network of interaction that reinforces the quality of each one. In fact, many so-called skills are simply ways of approaching tasks; they are reaction patterns that come from the same basic psychological, physical, emotional, and spiritual resources. These resources have been given to you by God, uniquely and individually, to make you special. As you get better, surer about using those resources—or developing those skills—you are cooperating in bringing to fullness a person God has designed and set free to make the world bloom.

God has supplied all the raw material you need to make the world work; how you develop and use it—whether toward the riches of material things or of the human spirit—is your part in creation. The work that you do with the skills you have is God's work as surely as it is your own, and perhaps more so. Earning a living, yes, but also much, much more!

N Clustering Your Skills

N ow take a look at the skill package you present. You've listed skills you *have* and *enjoy using*. And enjoy using in a variety of situations. They're adaptable, flexible. Marketable!

But what skills stand out on top? Which ones did you use in all five experiences listed on pages 55–59? Which in four? Three?

WORKSHEET 17

Go back to pages 55–59, count the skills you checked five times, and write them below. Indicate in which Skill Group (A–O) each belongs.

YOUR DOMINANT SKILLS   *SKILLS GROUP*
(checked FIVE times)

a. _____   _____

b. _____   _____

c. _____   _____

d. _____   _____

e. _____   _____

f. _____   _____

g. _____   _____

h. _____   _____

i. _____   _____

j. _____   _____

YOUR STRONG SKILLS   *SKILLS GROUP*
(checked FOUR times)

a. _____   _____

b. _____   _____

c. _____   _____
d. _____   _____
e. _____   _____
f. _____   _____
g. _____   _____
h. _____   _____
i. _____   _____
j. _____   _____

YOUR GOOD SKILLS   *SKILLS GROUP*
(checked THREE times)

a. _____   _____
b. _____   _____
c. _____   _____
d. _____   _____
e. _____   _____
f. _____   _____
g. _____   _____
h. _____   _____
i. _____   _____
j. _____   _____

Your Skill Profile

With your Dominant, Strong, and Good Skills listed, now blend them together into a clearer profile of the person ready to move into action.

WORKSHEET 18

1. You can find your place on the following list of worker
    profiles, characteristic patterns of action, or titles you
    might find on your door as others learn how you oper-
    ate. Using Worksheet # 17, count the total of A's you
    recorded, and enter that number next to THE PER-
    SUADER. Count the total of B's; enter the number
    next to THE ARTIST. And so on through the last pro-
    file, THE TREASURER.

Total
Score   *Profiles from Skill Groups*

A. THE PERSUADER. Getting people to act;
_____   winning and influencing; bringing people
           together; skills in communication of one
           kind or another; salesmanship; promotion.

B. THE ARTIST. Leaning toward one or more
_____   of the arts; usually tend to become
           engrossed in task; hate to be pressured,
           rushed; sensitive; able to be generous; not
           always practical.

C. THE MANAGER. Good at managing
_____   details, seeing the whole and its parts;
           generating cooperation; bringing order out
           of chaos; determining where to begin,
           knowing when to move on; seeing
           possibilities, creativity of a certain kind;
           planning.

D. THE COMMUNICATOR. Generally
_____   effective at writing, speaking; enjoy
           language; logical; respectful of detail; usually

steady, dependable; good at creating a whole from mixed bag of parts.

E.   THE EDUCATOR. Patience, perseverance; not burdened by repetition; good communication, listening skills; sensitive to persons, differences; willing to try different ways; goal-oriented; other-oriented.

F.   THE CREATOR. Imagination; sense of relationships; willing to risk; adaptable; often not detail-oriented; original in thinking, acting, producing; act easily on intuition; good memory.

G.   THE OBSERVER. Keen sense perception; careful, precise; attentive listener; able to size up people and situations quickly; may be somewhat judgmental; accurate; like facts; generally slow at decision-making but frequently on target.

H.   THE LEADER. Comfortable making decisions; perceptive; able to organize details, persons toward goals; usually some skill in communication, either directly or through choice of associates; move on without excessive afterthought; independent; self-directed.

I.   THE SCIENTIST. Sense of detail; value information; able to evaluate, diagnose, proceed in an orderly manner; generally patient, careful; not easily discouraged.

J.   NIMBLE FINGERS. Skills related to efficient hand work; good eye-hand coordination; mechanical sense; sense of spatial relations; ability to see parts and wholes; good sense of cause and effect; fine small-muscle control.

K. THE ATHLETE. Good large-muscle control; steadiness; endurance; energy; coordination; sense of adventure, perhaps of risk; open to challenge.

L. THE SUPPORT PERSON. Values accuracy, respects details; can be trusted to follow through; good memory and uses it well; punctual, good at following directions; can be trusted; works well under stress and in slower-paced situations; can be very loyal, keep confidences.

M. THE ENTERTAINER. Enjoys being center stage; usually has good sense of humor, sensitivity to audience/clients; good at influencing groups, public speaking; can be effective in public relations; may tend to be self-centered, emotional.

N. THE CARE-GIVER. Usually generous, hospitable, compassionate; people-oriented; gets along with a variety of people; can be very tolerant, patient, forbearing; remembers personal information well.

O. THE TREASURER. Comfortable with money, numbers, statistics; logical thinker; more inclined to things than people for energizing; may seek challenges; can think on his/her feet; not easily intimidated.

2. Now list these profiles, putting the one with the most checks first.

YOUR PROFILES   *TOTAL POINTS*

1. _____   _____
2. _____   _____
3. _____   _____
4. _____   _____
5. _____   _____
6. _____   _____
7. _____   _____
8. _____   _____
9. _____   _____
10. _____   _____
11. _____   _____
12. _____   _____
13. _____   _____
14. _____   _____
15. _____   _____

A Clearer Focus

It may be helpful to pay attention to the spread between points. If the spread is very small among two, three, or more profiles, you can see that the qualities of all those profiles show through your work. Remember, with an infinite variety of combinations of skills and capabilities, it is impossible to apply a single label to a real person.

If the point spread is very wide, the skills that dominate your activity are more pronounced in one or more particular category. You may need to give some thought to whether that reflects extreme virtuosity in certain skill areas—not a bad thing—or a possible overdevelopment in one area to the stunting of other areas.

Generally, your natural gifts and inclinations have a way of pushing themselves forward in the various situations of your life so that you do find chances to use them and thus develop the related skills. However, internal influences (sense of guilt, martyr syndrome, inadequate self-concept, etc.) and/or external influences (parental or authoritarian domination in formative years, limited environment, etc.) can contrive to create a lopsided developmental pattern. As you review your profile of skill development, think about the influences that have contributed to them. There may be some room for forgiveness and healing. There may be cause for praise and thanksgiving. Probably there should be a little of both.

Pondering a Bit

Live awhile with your skill profile. Pray, confer, read, and be attentive to the world around you. Identify ways in which the skill areas most evident in your successful and enjoyable experiences relate to one another. See how they dovetail in effective job performance and satisfaction for people around you who seem to be happy and positive about their work.

No profile is more important than any other; all are needed for the work of the Kingdom; all are meant to make human life more meaningful and whole. No combination of talents and skills is better than another; the marvelous variety of combinations is what makes each person unique, and all people delightful to discover in their abundant ways of being.

Take time to savor the extraordinarily fine and uniquely skilled person who lives within you.

Talking About It

Now that you have become acquainted with your unique skill package and with some of the additional potential within you for further development, you are in a stronger position to look at options, to set goals, and to tackle the job of finding a job—the job or career you really want. A later chapter is designed to help you in building your résumé, a portrait of yourself on paper. That résumé will get you some interviews, opportunities to fill in the portrait's fine lines and details face-to-face with an employer.

Now, however, would be a good time to familiarize yourself with the strengths of your Personal Skills Inventory, and also to make some preparations for the résumé and interview, by talking to yourself. Or to a friend. Or to your friendly tape recorder. But *talk*, don't write this one. Let's hear about you. The following questions are stimulators. Move beyond them. Get comfortable with sharing your strengths.

WORKSHEET 19

1. "Successful past experiences show that I am skilled in . . ." (What skill categories predominated in the Personal Skills Inventory? What skills within those categories are most evident? Most comfortable for you to dwell on? What specific experiences have demonstrated the use of these skills?)_____

_____

_____

_____

2. "I feel that I have some skill also in . . ." (Which skill areas are less pronounced but still have been somewhat

developed and would be comfortable to grow in? What experiences in relation to these skills have you learned from? How do you feel you could go about further developing these skills in the future?)_____

_____

_____

_____

_____

Reflecting with the Lord

Now you have completed the Getting-to-Know-You Inventory. Perhaps it simply reinforces what you already knew about yourself. Most people, however, find a few surprises. Spend a little prayerful time with your surprises. Fool around with them before the Lord.

Is God asking you to look at ways you've been guided along, perhaps without even being aware of it? Is God telling you that what you believed to be your greatest strengths are perhaps a little lower on the scale than you had thought? How have your employment responsibilities in the past corresponded to the skills you have used most successfully?

Some people give a pretty good impression, even to themselves, that they already know and accept their capabilities, skills, even weaknesses and faults very well—that it is comfortable and well-planned knowledge. The "got-it-together" people. But even those folks have a place inside, beyond the last chamber of their personal nautilus, where the uncertainty begins. That is the best place in the whole world. It's a place that the "got-it-together" people and the "all-over-the-wall" people actually have in common, a place where God and the human heart can meet on holy ground.

A willingness to walk into that place and dwell there for a while with God in the presence of your giftedness, your skills, and your life experiences is the step that means the most at this point. Only there can you come to terms with the more immediate question of "Where to next?" in your work life. The next job, career direction, or change of focus in your present job or career is a process, not a product. Take time to make haste slowly.

And take time to call that special friend and go out to dinner, or take a walk around the park, together. Talk it over with a person you trust, after you have first shared your reflections with the Lord. God and a caring, prudent friend can work together to help you recognize, learn to accept, and confirm your ability to act on the giftedness you carry around with you day in and day out.

CHAPTER 5

Values

Getting Below the Surface

In company with the self-putdown, aimlessness is one of the most debilitating of contemporary social afflictions.

Much ink has been spilled in recent years explaining the concept of "value" as essential to human experience. Motivation theory is utilized in all successful corporate enterprises. The whole phenomenon of Madison Avenue holds the nation, if not the world, in thrall with its efforts to harness the choice-power of the human person, that handle on the pot of gold at the end of the wallet.

It has been rightly said that you live what you value. Value exercise, and you find yourself jogging during the week, walking briskly to work or the grocery store, or signing up for aerobic classes; value good nutrition, and you'll pass up the grocery counter laden with creamy cheeses and chocolate brownies. Value honesty, and you might quit a job that looks productive to the outsider. If there is a *why* to live for, says Friedrich Nietzsche, one can bear with almost any *how*.

Identifying your values should not be difficult; simply observe the choices you make. That's a reasonable theory. The problem for many people is that too often the peace that should come from choices made in response to values is not there. Why? Several reasons could be:

1.   Values are not clear, so choices are made haphazardly and are not rooted in anything that will hold up in a storm.

2.   Values that are deep and solid are set aside, in favor of the more transient and the glittering, and thus the integration of lasting value and choice is blocked.

3.   Choices are sometimes made for people by circumstances they cannot even understand, much less control. Acting in response to a value is a luxury that many believe they cannot afford.

Values Determine Choices

But like it or not, values are at the heart of choices, and career choices most surely. If there is harmony among life values and life choices, there will be peace—not necessarily unassailable security, economic stability, unlimited achievement, but unquestionably peace. And right there is your list of values. You must weigh these values in coming to terms with choices about employment, work, career—however you name that part of your life that mirrors the creative energy of God.

The following activity invites you to spend some time with values that usually influence adult life satisfaction. The activity allows you to confront values with one another through the use of a grid, and to choose which, between any two, is the more significant to you *now*. Not which value used to be or which one ought to be, but which one *is* the more significant of the two. These values are not moral issues; one is not better than another. And if you're normal, the outcome of a personal analysis of these values will vary from year to year, from stage to stage of your life.

Own Your Values

To realign your work values from time to time, whether or not you are considering a career or job change, is a healthy, energizing thing to do. It can help keep you fine-tuned to your peak performance, personal satisfaction, and integrity. If peace of mind and heart is an ultimate value in career or job choice, this activity is a must.

Remember, it's not wrong to value a good salary and benefits, prestige and promotion on the career line. If these are the *only* work values you can claim, however, you are probably missing three fourths of the return possible from your days and years of work. You can—and many people do —integrate these values with others that spell satisfaction in another context. The more straightforwardly you can name and own *all* the values that are part of your decision-making in regard to work, the more validly your decisions will be made.

Personal Work Values

Move on, now, to look at your values. Study this list of Personal Work Values and their definitions. (Refer to this list as necessary while doing the exercise that follows.)

> #1   *Management/Supervision:* Being part of policy decisions; providing direction and accepting responsibility for the work of subordinates; being recognized as an authority.

#2   *Profit/Increased Income:* Salary, benefits, other compensation rising with continued job service; possibly moving toward part or total ownership or control.

#3   *Public Relations/Influencing Others:* Having ready contact with people outside place of work; opportunity for public interaction, limelight; marketing, sales.

#4   *Creativity:* Involvement in designing, developing, inventing, new/improved products, procedures, ideas, techniques. Having an idea ahead of the competition.

#5   *Location:* Being able to work in an area where you can live happily, do the things you want to do outside of work hours.

#6   *Leisure/Unpressured Situation:* Sense of casual accomplishment; little deadline pressure; productivity not measured by quotas; mental and physical space.

#7   *Variety/Excitement:* Characterized by tasks and responsibilities frequently changing; diversified situation; plenty of surprises; manageable crises; stimulation.

#8   *Family:* Situation allowing family responsibilities and priorities to be provided for; conditions appropriate to integrating work concerns and family concerns.

#9   *Stability/Job Security:* Assurance that you will have the job for as long as you continue to do the work; freedom from fear of layoffs, down-sizing, being bumped in reorganization.

#10   *Leadership:* Situation allowing you to take a forward-looking role in the organization; provide direction and plans for the future. Allowance for upward mobility within the structure; prestige, recognition for ideas and contributions to growth.

#11   *Independence/Set Own Agenda:* Flexibility of hours, work schedule. Being able to work alone when needed and desired; able to direct own work flow, set personal goals; minimum of supervision.

#12   *Civic Involvement/Community Service:* Situation allowing for active participation in your community and its issues. Encouragement of membership in, contribution to local government, nonprofit sector, charitable causes, community groups and projects.

#13   *Social Justice/Human Rights:* Work situation in which justice and human rights issues are openly addressed and espoused; justice in practice in the workplace as well as in policy statements.

#14   *Christian Environment:* Situation in which co-workers and associates are predominantly Christian, where religious observance is respected and even provided for; where decisions are made in a Christian value structure, and practices are similarly evaluated.

#15   *Detail/Precision Work:* Work allows for concentration and care; pride is taken in exactness and attention to detail; accuracy is valued and appreciated.

#16   *Learning/Personal Growth and Development:* Situation in which work allows for development of talents, refinement of skills, expansion of personal horizons; challenge to human potential within the individual; personal enrichment.

WORKSHEET 20

Having studied the preceding list of Personal Work Values and their definitions, look at the grid on page 78. You'll see that each of the sixteen values is listed twice: once down the page and once across the top. You will compare each one against every other one, step by step.

Making Your Choices, One by One

a. Start with #1 (Management/Supervision) on line one, compare it with #16 (Learning/Personal Growth and Development) from the list on top, and decide which of the two means more to you now. For example, if you were offered two jobs equally attractive in all areas, except that one offered more opportunity for management and supervision, and the other offered greater learning and personal growth —WHICH WOULD YOU CHOOSE?

b. Put that number—either #1 for Management/Supervision or #16 for Learning/Personal Growth—in the empty square where the two intersect on the grid.

c. Continue on across the page, *still on the first horizontal line,* and compare #1 (Management/Supervision) with the next value, #15 (Detail/Precision Work) on the vertical list. Which do you value more: #1 (Management/Supervision) or #15 (Detail/Precision Work)? Put your #1 OR #15 in this second empty square.

d. Compare Management/Supervision next with #14 (Christian Environment) and choose again the one you value most.

e. When you finish comparing Management/Supervision with all the other values, move to line 2, horizontally, and compare #2 (Profit/Increased Income) with each other value along the way.

Remember that the values listed are not moral issues; none is more "right" or "good" than another. Avoid laboring over a choice.

Counting Them Up

f.   When you have a number in every available square, count the number of times each value (#1–#16) has been selected on the ENTIRE GRID. Record the totals in the column marked "Frequency." Put the total number of 1's in the first space, opposite the first value, Management/Supervision. Put the total number of 2's in the empty space right below and opposite the second value, Profit/Increased Income; and so on. Count them all up and complete the Frequency column.

Listing Them in Sequence

g.   Find the value you've chosen the most times and put it in Space A under "Sequence of Values." Find the next highest choice and put it in Space B, and so on down the column. This Sequence of Values indicates the order in which you would, given a reasonable time and the mental space to do so, e-VALU-ate various possible career or job changes at this period of your life.

If you have chosen two values an equal number of times on the grid, go back to the square where these same two values meet or intersect. Which one did you choose earlier as your preference? That one is the more preferred of the two; put it in the higher spot in your Sequence column.

SOME BASIC WORK VALUES
TO COMPARE

	16. Learning/Personal Growth	15. Detail/Precision Work	14. Christian Environment	13. Social Justice/Human Rights	12. Civic Involvement/Community Service	11. Independence/Set Own Agenda	10. Leadership
1 Management/Supervision							
2 Profit/Increased Income							
3 Public Relations/Influencing Others							
4 Creativity							
5 Location							
6 Leisure/Unpressured Situation							
7 Variety/Excitement							
8 Family							
9 Stability/Job Security							
10 Leadership							X
11 Independence/Set Own Agenda						X	X
12 Civic Involvement/ Community Service					X	X	X
13 Social Justice/ Human Rights				X	X	X	X
14 Christian Environment			X	X	X	X	X
15 Detail/Precision Work		X	X	X	X	X	X
16 Learning/Personal Growth	X	X	X	X	X	X	X

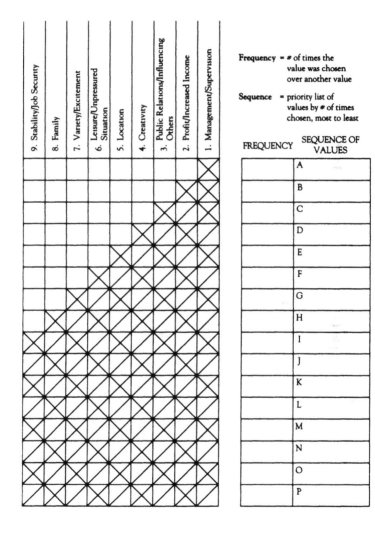

Frequency = # of times the value was chosen over another value

Sequence = priority list of values by # of times chosen, most to least

9.	Stability/Job Security
8.	Family
7.	Variety/Excitement
6.	Leisure/Unpressured Situation
5.	Location
4.	Creativity
3.	Public Relations/Influencing Others
2.	Profit/Increased Income
1.	Management/Supervision

FREQUENCY	SEQUENCE OF VALUES
	A
	B
	C
	D
	E
	F
	G
	H
	I
	J
	K
	L
	M
	N
	O
	P

Facing Values Head-on

Now that you have a representative overview of the values most likely to influence you in your job and career choices, where do you go with it? Most people find a good deal to ponder as they review their personal value hierarchy.

Sometimes it is difficult to admit that certain values are dominant right now. But to retreat from the truth is a sure path to confusion and lack of focus. And why retreat from accepting yourself where you are? Remember, none of the work values in the exercise are reprehensible; all have their place in everyone's work life to some degree. Their weight will vary with the years, the personal agendas you carry around, even the state of the stock market. What's important to you *is* important.

Some people are also concerned that certain values are low on their lists. They feel guilty. There is certainly a better approach to this kind of consideration, and that is a frank talk with the Lord about what it is you think you're guilty of. Is it something God is asking of you and you are refusing? Or is it something you are asking of yourself, demanding of yourself, while God is over on the sidelines waving wildly for you to look at what is really the Divine Will for you? God may be telling you things through your values grid that are truly freeing, truly peace-bringing for you. Let the good God who knows you and loves you anyway have a chance to make the point.

Whatever your prayer reveals as you review your work values, the exercise must be taken seriously as you search for the right work situation. It is vital that you respect your strong values as you investigate new career paths and send out résumés. Failure to do so will block your progress. You'll find a stalemate at every step. So trust your instincts. Trust the God who cares how it goes with you. And don't be afraid to risk accepting yourself just as you are right now.

CHAPTER 6

Getting It All Together

W hen is your self-assessment complete and your future direction assured? About forty-five minutes after the cessation of the heartbeat, if you're a member of the human race.

Part of the fun of human living is the continuing process of self-discovery. Change, or growth, is our special mission, a fascinating journey toward the wonderful "Aha!" that will be our personal, unique moment of truth before God.

If you had done your skills and values assessments ten years ago, or five, or possibly even one, they could have indicated different things rather than what they did now. When you review these processes in another place and time in your life, there will be some new information for you to work with. No matter who you are or what you've done, you aren't finished yet!

Even the great "Aha!" spoken of earlier, that face-to-face with the God you've been trying for so long to get to know, cannot really be viewed as "The End." Life with God beyond time must surely be as delightfully open to surprises as the life you lead with God here in time. Will there be more to unfold, more to savor about yourself forever? Why not?

T Skills and Values Make You YOU

The last activity in this section invites you to look back quietly over the work you have done thus far, in comfortable dialogue with your God, who was, after all, doing the work with you. Let yourself relax in God's presence, and vice versa, to talk it over.

Your career search means more to you than finding a job, earning a higher salary, satisfying a need for prestige. It means more to you than that or you wouldn't be reading this book. You believe, and rightly so, that what you choose to do with your work days and years, no matter how prestigious or quiet, is an integral part of the person you are. It's important to you that you are carrying out your special mission, your place in God's plan, peacefully and joyfully in the day-to-day work you do.

So begin that conversation with the Lord you love. If it's helpful, write your side of the conversation in the workspace provided here. These questions may guide your reflection.

WORKSHEET 21

1. Do you appreciate and accept the gifts God has given you? Or are you still agonizing over those God has given to others? How do you live your thanks for *your own* gifts?_____

    _____

    _____

    _____

    _____

2. How has God been with you as you have grown in "wisdom, age, and grace"? How do you know God's caring presence has been part of your life story?_____

_____
_____
_____
_____
_____

3. Are you ready to offer back to God the skills you have developed, using them in daily work that will help you and others to live more fully human, Christian lives?

_____
_____
_____
_____
_____

4. What are your honest feelings about the direction of your career path at this point in your life? Can you trust that God has been with you in what, to you, were the best of times and the worst of times? Can you trust that God continues to have a plan in which your particular talents, skills, and experiences play an important part?

_____
_____
_____
_____
_____

5. Do you have an idea of the kinds of employment that will help you to serve God, yourself, and others well during the next stage of your life?_____

_____
_____
_____
_____
_____

6. What do you ask of God at this time? What do you
   really want? What does God ask of you?_____

   _____

   _____

   _____

   _____

   _____

How Do You
Prepare? Attitudes

Out of his infinite glory, may he give you the power for your hidden self to grow strong, so that Christ may live in your hearts through faith. . . . Glory be to him whose power working in us, can do infinitely more than we can ask or imagine

Ephesians 3:16, 20

It's the proverbial glass half full of water—or half empty. Or the doughnut and the hole. Or the old farmer who hadn't been to town in quite a spell, and was puzzled to see people wearing jeans—men, women, and children. "Didn't know things were as bad as they is," he said. "Nobody's got money enough to buy good clothes these days. They're ALL wearin' overalls!"

It depends on your viewpoint or attitude. If you can't change the circumstances, as the old adage advises, change the way you react to them.

So when life is a bit tense, and segments of it fly apart; when a career change looks good but the risks might be too high; when pressures prevent that sense of wholeness you crave—the right attitude can help bring things together.

It's the glue that puts the parts where they belong and thus brings the whole picture into focus. The right attitude is often the cause for success and the remedy for failure. It won't stop the rain, type your final draft, or repair the lawn mower. But it might make those pesky problems a little less pesky.

It won't alter the need for a change in the job or the job description, salary scale, or employer. But it probably will change YOU.

So, start with yourself. How long has it been since you've had top priority, since your needs were "front stage, center"? Maybe you've overlooked some basic "mental musts" that can help to highlight your worth, such as the following:

- You're a whole person with unique interests.
- It's okay to have "druthers" or preferences.
- You're worth it—and a whole lot more.
- Treats keep you going and you deserve them.
- Sharing your journey is a plus.
- Staying honest gives you energy.
- Bite-sizing your goals builds confidence.

Exercises in this section are designed to help you put it all together by keeping *yourself* all together! But use them one by one, every day or so. And don't plow through, head down, determined to finish at breakneck speed.

Take your time. Happily discern that great person hidden inside your skin. Choose your treats and check your track record; bite-size your goals and share your journey. EXPECT success and you're on your way!

CHAPTER 7

The Whole Person

You're not a robot or a machine; you're a real, on-the-way human being. And an employer hires the whole person—the entire you. Get in touch with some of the refinements of this complex and unique job-seeker before you look at job openings, prepare résumés, and go for interviews. Own your many and varied interests; you're an *interesting* person.

WORKSHEET 22

This exercise will give you more confidence in the person you take into the job interview. Fill in the blanks in the following statements; or, if you prefer, do this exercise out loud with a friend. Be honest with yourself.

  a. When you have a free afternoon, you like to _____

  b. You feel most energized and renewed when you _____

  c. Some of your favorite ways to treat yourself are _____

d. You find the best ways to relax are _____

e. You wish you could _____ because _____

f. Your tastes in music/reading/art/entertainment run to _____

g. You wish you owned/had access to _____ because _____

h. Someone you admire very much is _____ because _____

i. If you could get additional education, you'd most likely study _____ because _____

j. Publications/magazines you most enjoy reading are

_____

k. Activities that renew your energy and zest for living are _____

l. The most personally rewarding thing you did this past month was _____

Get the picture? No one else is quite like you. No one! As an old Russian proverb says, "If I try to be like him or her, who will be like me?"

"Druthers"

It's okay liking to work alone or with a team, outside or inside or up in the attic. It's okay to have a fondness for statistics or to want to meet the customers coming in the front door. And it's okay to settle for a noncompetitive job that fits your profile. Not everyone wishes to reach the top rung of the so-called ladder of success. Maybe for you, rung number six is just fine—and true success.

Wanda's Story

Wanda became a nurse and longed to be floor supervisor. Whereas she loved working with patients, carried her special smile into each hospital room, and had the "human touch," she craved that Supervisor name tag. After several seasons of success as a regular nurse, she applied for a job as head of the pediatrics floor. She got the job; her goal had been reached. But less than a year later, Wanda turned in the Supervisor tag. Working with patients and comforting parents gave her energy and life; supervising involved too many tasks she disliked. She may have stepped "down" on the so-called ladder, but she stepped "up" to her potential.

Your Submerged Self

In your past experience, you may have generously submerged personal preferences in favor of family need and enjoyment, or other motivation—even when the cost was high to yourself. Because of this past generosity, you might find it difficult to articulate any preferences you may have in the workplace, or even to admit you have them.

Yet life asks for your mature, intelligent cooperation in the employment process. A spouse, a family, and you yourself are best served when your employment matches *your* needs and preferences.

Your Dream Job

This exercise invites you to get in touch honestly and simply with the job you'd like to have. Call it your "Dream Job." Spell it out in as much detail as you can. Allow your spirit to feel peace, joy, satisfaction in service and in professional excellence—whatever is best among the rewards of labor for those you love, and for the Lord.

WORKSHEET 23

What does that Dream Job look like?

Job Title _____

Employer _____

Location _____

Hours/Schedule _____

Co-workers _____

Responsibilities _____

Work Environment _____

Supervisors _____

Salary/Benefits _____

Support Services/Equipment _____

WORKSHEET 24

After a day or two, go back over this Dream Job prayerfully and slowly. Consider what would be most *important and valuable* to you in a work situation. Sort it out: the ideal from the next best thing.

1. Draw a big star on Worksheet # 23 alongside those items you *really need and want* in a job or career change. Copy here what you give top priority:

    a. _____

    b. _____

    c. _____

2. Now, on the same worksheet, circle those you'd find desirable—those that would be beneficial but not essential. Their lack would not seriously interfere with your effectiveness, health, or happiness.
Copy those desirable Dream Job aspects here:

a. _____

b. _____

c. _____

3. There! You've got a handle on what you'd like to have. Now put your essential and desirable factors together:

List A: Essential	List B: Beneficial and Desirable
a. _____	_____
b. _____	_____
c. _____	_____

Even though few ever find their Dream Job, you now know what yours looks like. It fits YOU. And the job you seek or the change you ponder should have at least some of your essentials and more than a few of your "desirables."

CHAPTER 8

You're Worth It

The job search can be draining physically, emotionally, spiritually. If you're a serious job-seeker, you need a self-care plan to replenish the personal resources you need to carry on with your "work," your search for employment.

Your Personal Needs

Take time to take care. You're the only YOU you've got —the only you lots of people love. Listen to your inner self and be sure it's being nourished.

This next exercise is intended to help you highlight some danger signals—some attitudes that scuttle progress and growth. Jot them down. *They are important.*

WORKSHEET 25

When you are depressed, tired, discouraged, what signs indicate this?

To Yourself	*To Others (ask them)*
_____	_____
_____	_____
_____	_____
_____	_____
_____	_____

Maybe you need some treats, a listening ear, more attainable goals, or a "staying-honest plan." Peeking ahead, you'll find some more attitude changers—take your pick!

Treats!

What will it be? Cold lemonade or hot tea? A good book or a brisk walk? Browsing in the hardware store, fixing that screen door, knitting a few more rows, playing bingo, or jogging through the park?

Everyone's list will be different, but have your own fun-to-do items "pre-thought." You'll have no excuse for not following through when a treat is needed.

Your Choice

Make a list of treats you give yourself, or could give yourself, that

1. are healthful.

2. are within your budget.

3. will not interfere with your ordinary obligations or your current job-search task.

Here are a few typical treats you might claim as your own:

- Soak in a nice, fragrant bubble bath or take a long, warm shower.
- Write a note to an old friend or relative (you might get one back).
- Have tea or coffee at a restaurant with a view.
- Call someone you love to talk with.
- Visit a pet shop and play with the puppies.
- Check a good book out of the library.
- Browse for an hour at your favorite store.
- Get a haircut.
- Pack a snack sack and go walking to a favorite spot.
- Buy yourself a little present.
- Sleep late tomorrow morning.

(Be creative. Vary your goodies. Don't make them all edible!)

WORKSHEET 26

1. What's on *your* treat list?

a. _____

b. _____

c. _____

d. _____

e. _____

f. _____

g. _____

h. _____

i. _____

j. _____

2. Use your treat list in the way that's effective for you. You might:
   a. Treat yourself when you've finished your job search plan for the day or week.
   b. Treat yourself whenever a prospect ends with a "no."
   c. Treat yourself at 3 P.M. every afternoon when you're on duty searching.

CHAPTER 9

Making the Journey Easier

Y ou may remember the touching story of the boy who arrived at Boys Town years ago on a cold night. When questioned about the bundle he was carrying, the lad answered, "He's not heavy. He's my brother."

Burdens Shared

B urdens shared are burdens lightened. So decide on one or more persons with whom you can share your job search. Persons who are accessible, who care about you, who have good judgment and common sense. List a few possibilities here:

WORKSHEET 27

NAMES   WHY?

1. _____   _____

2. _____   _____

3. _____   _____

4. _____   _____

The Pact

W hen you've decided who you'd like your fellow traveler(s) to be, ask them if they will journey with you. You will make a pact with them that goes something like this:

"I'm going to be searching for employment during the next few weeks or months. I would like to share my efforts and progress with you as I go along. You don't need to make decisions for me or give advice, although your advice would be valuable.

"What I do need from you is your support and encouragement, and also feedback on how you see me progressing. Tell me if I seem moody or depressed, if I am maintaining a healthy balance in my thinking and activity. Tell me if you think I am not being practical or prudent, and tell me why.

"I don't know how long it will be before I find employment, but the right thing will come. In the meantime, I will appreciate your sharing my work with me. My work right now is to find employment."

Arrange times to meet or phone. Perhaps you can build these visits into your own treat plan, because they *should* be treats.

Staying Honest

There's nothing like a good, clear mirror to reflect the twinkle in your eye—and expose the wrinkle just arrived! Most mirrors are honest. So, too, is a check-up like the following on what's occurring in your life.

At least once a week (choose a regular day and time—e.g., Sunday evening), review your health and welfare. Use this page for a brief notation each time. This will help prevent creeping disintegration from taking over on the sly.

WORKSHEET 28

Date	Weight	Average Hrs Sleep	Type/Amount Exercise	Nutrition	Corrective Action (if any needed)

1. What do you see that you like? _____

2. What needs changing? _____

_____

_____

Bite-Sizing Your Goals

Once in a famous comic strip, a rookie was at bat. "Strike three!" He strikes out again and slumps to the bench, saying "Rats! I'll never be a big-league player. I just don't have it. All my life I've dreamed of playing in the big leagues, but I know I'll never make it." A "helpful" team member turns to console him: "You're thinking too far ahead. What you need to do is to set yourself more immediate goals." He asks, "Immediate goals?" "Yes," she replies. "Start with this next inning when you go out to pitch. See if you can walk out to the mound without falling down."

Success Along the Way

Good advice for all: bite-size your goals. While success in your job search may be slow in coming, you can have many smaller successes along the way if you divide and conquer. Set for yourself *monthly, weekly,* even *daily* goals that are realistic, positive, satisfying. Here's an example:

Goal for Month One:
- to complete all necessary personal records you'll need for résumés and applications
- to complete all preparation exercises in this book
- to meet with your journey-partner(s) each week as planned
- to send out fifteen letters of inquiry, and schedule at least ten follow-up visits to explore possibilities and

let key people know you're available (See "Networking" in Chapter 11).

* to prepare a general résumé focused on your strongest skill area

WORKSHEET 29

1. Use this space to line up your initial goals when you decide you're ready for a change of job or career.

GOALS FOR MONTH ONE

a. _____

b. _____

c. _____

d. _____

e. _____

Your Track Record

Break these goals down into four weekly goal packages. In some instances, you might want to set some daily goals, especially if you tend to be a procrastinator. And remember your *treats!*

1. Try using a calendar with room to write on for breaking down monthly goals into weekly/daily goals. (See Planning Guide in Appendix, page 260.)
2. At the end of each week, assess your progress.
3. Revise goals if you haven't been realistic. (This is good material to go over with a support person or group.)

4. Give yourself credit for what you have accomplished. Include one of your treats!

5. Revise the next week's goals appropriately.

At the beginning of the fourth week, set your goals for the following month. There's nothing like scratching out a task that's been completed or checking off a goal that's been achieved. If you find that you rarely or never accomplish a goal, chances are your goals are unrealistic for the time and resources available. The bites are choking you. Cut the pieces smaller until you do find yourself making steady—not perfect but steady—progress. Mountains are climbed inch by inch; career changes are made step by step.

The Christian Attitude

As Christians, "We know that by turning everything to their good God co-operates with all those who love him, with all those that he has called according to his purpose." (Rom 8:28) A hard Scripture to live by? Yes. But deep down, this attitude builds the basis for success.

By integrating your interests, your "druthers," and your self-worth while sharing the journey, staying honest, and bite-sizing your goals, you break down barriers—barriers and boxes that keep you fragmented and frustrated.

Choosing your treats and checking your track record, you can face the future as a whole human person with skills and goals, with needs and preferences.

With all these elements put together, so that you feel positive and ready, you turn to the job market and see where you—the unique you—can best use your gifts and talents in meaningful employment. The next section invites you to look at where the jobs are.

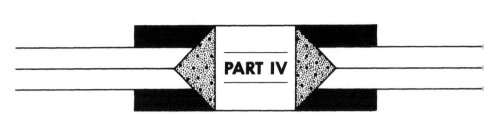

PART IV

Where Are the Jobs? Resources and Methods

So I say to you: Ask, and it will be given to you; search, and you will find; knock, and the door will be opened to you For the one who asks always receives; the one who searches always finds; the one who knocks will always have the door opened.

Luke 11:9–11

So you've determined that a change in your work life is in order. You've decided who you are and what direction you want to take. Now, where's the job?

Here's where the big chill comes in! Unless you're lucky enough to be the son or daughter of a company president, you face the wide world of employment—a vast no-one's land of strange and transient faces populating personnel offices, employment agencies, and bulletin board "spaces-in-front-of."

This search can be a truly rewarding and productive time. You're a learner, researcher, explorer. A spirit of adventure and challenge enters the picture at this point. The job search itself—discovering what and where the jobs are—has often been a whole life turn-around for "ho-hum" careers.

Actually, getting a job *is* a job. A serious career-shaping venture that will sharpen your skills, expand your vision, and help fulfill your God-given potential. It can bring out the creativity, imagination, and recessive talents within you.

Expect the job of job searching to be challenging and energizing. In fact, you may be just a little disappointed if an unexpected employment opportunity that looks just perfect falls your way before you've had a chance to explore the field. You'll be missing an opportunity for growth.

It's also important to remember that the range and number of jobs out there for you are going to be, in general, closely related to the range and number of needs, demands, and expectations you have. The narrower your focus about what work you will do, what compensation you will accept, and where you will reside, the narrower your base of available openings. Circumstances outside your control, such as your family size and physical condition, may dictate some aspects of your employment-opportunity base. But many aspects are within your control. What "give" are you willing to allow in your job search? What "give" might the Lord be urging you to consider in order to bring about His will in your life? As you pursue your exploration, be sensitive to the continuing tension between your legitimate self-interest and the urgings of the Spirit.

What about it? Are you open to new possibilities? Can you see the forest *and* the trees? What kind of trees are out there anyway? Where and how do you look for the jobs?

This section is designed to help you sort out the resources and the methods that effective job-seeking entails.

CHAPTER 10

The Resources

You are by no means alone in either your career search or your tackling the job market. And most communities of any size have resources to help. Ferret them out and use them as they fit your needs. What's there to lose?

Local Colleges

Local colleges and universities have well-planned programs to help both students and non-students explore their career potential and the local job scene. Career counseling, computerized assessment and referral services, value-clarification workshops, short courses and seminars, and testing programs—many free or at very low cost—are standard features at most colleges, particularly community and state institutions. The increasing appeal to these schools of the mature potential student as a supplement to their dwindling undergraduate rosters has given impetus to these services. Use them!

In addition, many colleges offer credit for verified work experience that coordinates with various academic tracks. Your on-the-job experience is invaluable education and is recognized as such by employers who usually look first at performance in the field, then at degrees and GPAs, when reviewing résumés.

Community Groups

Other job-search resources to explore in your community include community and neighborhood centers, YM- and YWCAs, and state, county, and city employment support programs. Many public libraries maintain excellent resource materials, both computerized and print, to assist local populations both of employers and of job-seekers. Some libraries even offer workshops, referral assistance, and open bulletin boards to help you network for career enhancement.

Churches

An increasingly common response of churches to the practical human needs of their congregations involves employment assistance. Help in clarifying values and skills, and in discerning God's will in daily work, can be found among church adult education offerings and outreach services. Some churches provide job banks and job counseling, as well as retreats and workshops devoted to job searching for their own members and for others who turn to them in hope.

Placement Services

Private counselors and placement services are also available if you prefer to use them, but check them for reliability and qualifications before commitments—which can sometimes be costly—are made. Be aware, too, that employment agents have their own quotas to fill, and may try to encourage you to accept a position you're unsure of or don't want altogether. Watch out for "gentle persuasion"!

These resources can, however, provide excellent one-on-one service in helping you match your skills and experience with the local job market. They help, too, if you encounter some of the many potential roadblocks to peace and progress in your career search—such as anxiety, depression, poor self-image, inappropriate goals, and family stress.

The Grapevine

Don't overlook the internal grapevine at your present workplace or in the neighborhood. A large company or organization with continuing turnover regularly creates new openings. How are these publicized? Personnel office memos? Bulletin boards? In-house newsletters? Unless you are certain that you need a complete change of scene, look under your nose first. Hiring from within is a common form of company employment, contributing to the employees' career development or advancement and saving an employer the costs and productivity involved in training new employees.

The at-home job seeker can make contacts as well. Tell the mail carrier and the grocery clerk, your dentist, doctor, and neighbors down the street, that you're looking for a job. Inform your cousins, Uncle Joshua, and your minister.

Publications/Hot Lines

Be alert to magazines and professional publications relating to your fields of competence and interest; networking and placement offices in your diocese or professional society; job-clearing houses; employment hot-lines (often maintained by hospitals, universities, corporations, or other mega-employers) providing twenty-four-hour recorded services with updated information; and local and out-of-town newspaper classified advertising.

What You'll Learn

What will you learn from these resources? First, you'll learn that there are lots of jobs you can do and lots of jobs you never knew existed. Secondly, you'll discover more about the required qualifications for work that interests and attracts you. And you'll begin to zero in, if necessary, on skill weaknesses that may keep you from the job you want.

You'll also refine your awareness of current salary ranges and the tight or loose condition of the job market; and learn where you'll most likely gain a foothold versus where you'll face formidable obstacles in your job seeking.

Job resources do more than just list available openings. They're the key to the whole employment pattern in your own geographical area, professional field, or particular situation—invaluable in developing long-term, coordinated plans for your career progress.

And that kind of planning fits into the bigger picture of how God is calling you over the years to live out your best gifts through your work experience. A time of job transition, when you are motivated to seek out and concentrate intensely on job-finding resources, is also a time when the Spirit can be most active in your life. Tune in!

Using Resources Near You

Here are some exercises to help you discover and organize local job-search resources.

WORKSHEET 30

Fill out this sheet to get an overview of the resources available to you now.

Service/ Resource Program	Sponsor & Location	Services Offered	Cost/ Qualifi- cation	Contact Phone/ Hours
Example:				
State Employ- ment Security Office	State 1608 West Main St.	Job openings salary data	Free	Mon-Fri. 8:00–5:00 624-6090

Using Job Companies and Private Resources

If you have not worked with a private employment agency or counselor before, this worksheet might help you determine if you wish to use such a resource. Check your local telephone directory under Employment for agencies in your locale. Call and "interview" a representative, using this worksheet as a guide. Under Counselors or Counseling, you will find agencies or individuals who may specialize in career issues; try a telephone interview here, too. Then decide if any of these services are right for you.

WORKSHEET 31

1. What services do you offer to an individual interested in (career change, improving employment situation, finding a new job)? _____

   _____

   _____

   _____

   _____

2. What are your fees? When payable? _____

   _____

   _____

   _____

   _____

3. What are your qualifications? _____

   _____

   _____

   _____

   _____

4. What are your hours of service? _____

   _____

   _____

_____

_____

5. What do you find to be the average time in weeks or months that a client is involved with your services before securing a new position? _____

_____

_____

_____

_____

6. After a job or career change has been made, do you do any follow-up to determine the effectiveness of the change? _____

_____

_____

_____

_____

CHAPTER 11

The Methods

Job search is most productive when it uses a variety of approaches simultaneously. The following are suggested for their proven effectiveness and their ability to support one another:

- Networking
- Canvassing
- Volunteering
- Entrepreneuring

A little exploration of how each one works will give you the larger picture. So don't give up now; the next few pages may strike a resonant chord in your head or heart. Or both. The Spirit is working with you!

Networking: Steve's Story

Networking is another word for fishing—with a whole bunch of lines out at the same time. It involves linking your job availability with a variety of personal contacts—relatives, friends, associates, professionals, tradespeople—whose own contacts can increase your sphere of shared information.

Steve, a recent graduate, had been looking for a job and nothing seemed to be coming down the pike that fit his interests and training. One weekend, he joined his former roommate Pete on a quick jaunt across the state to visit Pete's parents. Arriving late Friday night, the two young men were enjoying the luxury of Mom and Dad's hospitality. "What kind of job are you looking for, Steve?" Pete's father asked. After obtaining a few brief facts about Steve's degree and skills, he said, "I know a friend looking for just that kind of background. . . ." And although it sounds like a "happily ever after" ending, Steve got the job he had first heard about around the kitchen table while enjoying some homemade apple pie!

Sharing

Actually, networking is something you can do at any time; it's not peculiar to the job search. Sharing your professional growth, your work success, your satisfaction with what you are doing should be part of ordinary, healthy interaction with those you care about.

We hear a lot these days about faith sharing. Where is faith in God's day-to-day action in your life more evident than in those significant hours you spend in honest labor? God is there—wants to be there. If you are accustomed to talking comfortably about your work life with family and friends—not griping about the boss or complaining about co-workers—you can discover remarkable things about the

God who works shoulder to shoulder with you. And the people you share with can discover the kind of worker you are—something important when it comes to job or career change and you need their support, insight, counsel, or prayer.

Connecting

1. Before you are "between jobs," begin your phone calls, letters, and/or personal visits.

2. Realize that you are seeking not a job but information; you are looking for suggestions, and leads to persons, companies, and the like that are related to your fields of interest and competence.

3. "Picking brains" will give you valuable information about both your future job search and your present endeavors.

4. As you develop your list of contacts, make appointments to talk with them briefly or send short notes to set up meetings. They might go like this:

    > I am particularly interested in learning more about [field/company]. In a recent conversation with [name your friend, relative, or other contact], (s)he suggested I contact you to discuss your work in this [field/company]. Before next week, I will call to set a time convenient for you when we can meet.
    >
    > I look forward to talking with you and hearing about your successful work in [field/company].

5. When you visit, be prepared. Have some good questions about the company, the work you're most interested in doing, trends in the field. Know some-

thing about the person you'll be speaking with so that a friendly tone can be established.

6. Keep your visit brief and express your appreciation for the time given.

7. Send a (typewritten) thank-you note afterward.

8. Review key points given in Chapter 15 for more information about these short "interviews."

Sharing and connecting, the two major elements in networking that have just been discussed, can: 1) provide helpful insights and data to round out your information base when actual job-search time comes; and 2) they plant a positive image of yourself in the awareness of people who may have further helpful contacts.

One caution, however: don't be a pest. Use good judgment. A strong, integrated first impression gives a head start in the job search. Quiet, unpretentious reinforcement of that first impression does not a hurt a bit.

For example, call someone you talked with last week at Company A about a good speaker or an in-service program. This call keeps communication open and underscores your own interest in professional updating. Together with a personal note, send someone from Company B an article relevant to your conversation with him or her. This contact brings to mind your name and the value you placed on the interview. Space such contacts judiciously, vary the type of contacts, and always make them at times and in ways convenient for the person addressed. Pestering and ungainly reminders that "Here I am!" will give negative signals.

The following worksheet suggests some questions that might be asked on a networking visit. You're invited to add others that would be pertinent to your concerns.

WORKSHEET 32

Some questions you might ask at a networking visit include:

a. What growth patterns do you see in this field (area, industry, etc.)?
b. Where are you finding the greatest needs in your personnel? For example, in specializations, in-service training, general experience?
c. What qualities do you see as most important to successful work in this field (institution, industry, etc.)?
d. How did you yourself become interested in this work?
e. What are some of the most significant problems you face at the present time in maintaining quality service?
f. Add your own well-thought-out questions pertaining to your field of interest:

- _____
- _____
- _____
- _____
- _____

Of course, you'll take a small notebook for recording important ideas you get during your visits; this will prove helpful in preparing for subsequent visits and you'll discover that with practice your questions will become more on target.

Someone who knows and asks a few really good questions is more valuable to an intelligent employer than the person who behaves as if he or she has ALL the answers!

Are you ready now to make a list of contacts? Use the next worksheet to help gather all that information swimming around in your head.

WORKSHEET 33

1. Use this worksheet to begin a list of personal contacts you might approach in the preliminary stages of your job search. You may refine the list as you determine specific employment targets.

2. For starters, shoot the works: former employers and co-workers, relatives, friends, people in your church, professionals and service people (your family doctor, dentist, hairdresser, etc.), teachers (past and present), members of organizations you belong to (e.g., the bowling team), and persons you know through community affairs and social activities. Write names of anyone you know and could comfortably approach to ask about recommending contacts in your field of work:

Your Personal Contact	Phone #	Contacts Recommended and Why
Example:		
Dr. Gamble	425-9896	Rita Morales, general manager of Worldwide Travel. Lots of experience in travel business. Hires local agents. Formerly with Sutton Travel Agency.
Pastor Lang	987-3421	Mary Ruth Blake. Travel agent experience. Now does private group organizing out of own home. Member of my church.
a. _____		

b. _____

_____

_____

_____

c. _____

_____

_____

_____

d. _____

_____

_____

_____

e. _____

_____

_____

_____

f. _____

_____

_____

_____

_____

Canvassing

A time-honored technique for ferreting out a job is the canvass. Basically, this method encompasses either a *geographical region*—if working in a certain place is of prime importance to you—or an *employment field*—if location is not important. A few basics will give you the picture.

Materials

1. You'll need an attractive general résumé highlighting your strengths, achievements, and potential. (You'll

find a ready-made example of a general, nonfocused
résumé on page 148.)

2. You'll also need a good cover letter that sets the
stage:

> I am investigating (area, industry, etc.) in prep-
> aration for a change in employment. . . .

> I am open to possibilities for which you might
> consider my skills and experience suit-
> able. . . .

> I value your knowledge of the (area, industry,
> etc.) and would appreciate your sharing my in-
> terest with others in management positions.

A sample cover letter is found on page 183.

3. A list of addresses developed from directories (e.g.,
the Chamber of Commerce, special interest groups
or services) may form the core of your canvass. The
public library can help you find directories pertinent
to your needs. Trade journals, house or corporation
listings, and professional societies can help, too.

4. Names and titles of individuals you'll send your
packet to must be exact. Contacting the manager or
personnel director by name can take your résumé
right to the one who does the hiring. You more
readily open junk mail if it's addressed to *you*; mail
sent to "Occupant" or "Resident" doesn't entice us
that much! So too with employers. Know the name
and go for the top! And spell it correctly—even if
you must make a long distance call to verify that
Fredrick Ferguson, Personnel Director, spells his
Fredrick without an "e."

Procedures

1. If local directory resources are insufficient for distant targets, perhaps a friend or relative in those locales can help you find key prospects. Or call the Chamber of Commerce, professional societies, union offices and such. If you connect with a friendly native at such a central source of up-to-date information, you might pick up valuable side tips on where the market is, who's the best/biggest employer, or new developments coming down the road. Store your new-found "scuttlebutt" for future use.

2. Develop a simple filing system for data you'll obtain through your canvass; three-by-five-inch cards will do. For each target, record the following:

   • to whom mailing was addressed (including title)

   • date sent

   • any response

   • any follow-up phone contact or visit made; date and outcome

   • further contacts obtained from *this* target

3. Canvassing should be ongoing, so continue researching appropriate targets steadily, adding to your file as you go.

4. Keep a supply of résumés on hand. Have your matching cover letters and envelopes ready for individualizing with new names and addresses.

5. Follow up with a call a few days after your packet has arrived at its destination. Avoid calling on Mondays, Fridays, or the day before a holiday. Ask for the person to whom you sent your résumé; if he or she is not available, ask when you might call back. Do not

go into detail about your job interest with the receptionist, secretary, or whoever answers the phone.

6. When you do reach your "target person," include
the following in your conversation:

- interest in the company, agency, institution, etc.

- an inquiry: Did you receive my résumé and cover
letter?

- a few questions or comments demonstrating
knowledge of the field, as well as interest in
what's going on and in the potential for job
openings

- expression of appreciation for the conversation
and desire to keep in contact

7. Be brief, letting your "target" take the lead in the
timing. If he or she indicates interest in knowing
more about you, don't get tongue-tied. A positive
canvass call has led to more than one interview and
good position!

8. Remain positive. This is no time to suggest that
you're bothering a busy person or that you're sure
there are no openings just now. Why bother if you're
going to slash yourself in the first thirty seconds of
your call?

People sometimes have a hard time making the follow-up
because they are "shy." You are capable of much if you have
the desire. To be more confident, you might want to rehearse with a reliable friend just to hear your own voice and
discover how you react to a person whose response you cannot predict.

Managers, supervisors, and company presidents are
members of the human race. As professionals, generally,
they are courteous, and they are interested in maintaining
high quality in their operations. Be aware of these factors

when calling. You're not, after all, looking for a job so much as offering them an opportunity. With every call, you will gain confidence and leave your mark of distinction with a new acquaintance who may, in time, become a friend.

Volunteering: Beth's Story

Some studies say that as many as 70 to 80 percent of job openings are hidden—that is, never actively advertised to the general public—because there is no need to advertise them. Appropriate candidates are readily at hand. So, aside from whatever listing formalities are necessary for corporations to conform with law or with company policies, the hiring can be very much an "at home" affair.

Because these jobs are hidden, you are well advised to "make friends with the mammon of iniquity" and become recognizable in areas where your future employment might be desirable.

In fields where budgets are tight—social service, church and religious work, and the arts, for example—volunteer work is an ideal "way in." And with so many cutbacks in recent years, finding enterprises with squeezed budgets isn't difficult at all.

Feeling that a change was coming in her firm's management, Beth realized she needed to be prepared for the organizational shift a new boss would probably bring.

Beth liked her work as executive secretary and found it relaxing after years of classroom teaching and school administration that had all but burned her out. Still, she missed the challenges of education—the interaction with children, parents, other educators. Something deep in the blood, she said, laughing, to her friends.

One day Beth heard a chance remark about a new program at the county mental health center, a program looking for volunteers to work with emotionally disturbed children and specially trained foster families. She responded to the invitation, attended some training sessions, and was given an assignment to help the foster parents with respite care on specified evenings and weekends.

Beth's background in education, though, soon brought her into more contact with casework staff as they labored to assist the foster parents with school-related issues. These were hard kids to fit into classroom settings—disruptive, defensive, hurting kids. Beth's understanding of placement and support problems from the teacher's point of view was a revelation to the casework staff; parents began asking her to go with them to conferences with their children's teachers. Caseworkers began asking her opinion on proposed school placements prior to accepting a new child. In one stubborn case, the program director asked Beth to spend time observing the child at school to help them gain further insight into his problems.

A year into the new program, when grants were being written for continued funding, the staff and program director, not to mention foster parents, were openly asking the mental health center to create a position for an educational specialist. Beth's natural gifts for working well with people and her experience and skills as a teacher had made her all but indispensable to successful case management.

By this time, Beth's new boss, as anticipated, had made his own plans for office reorganization, and Beth was able to resign gracefully. Then, with her knowledge of the mental health field, the team spirit that had developed with the professionals she worked with, and the assurance of her own professional competence, she stepped into a new but related career.

Benefits

Volunteering is a great way to get to know the organization, see things first-hand, and discover whether you'd really like to work *there,* or—in the case of contemplated career change—in the field at all.

Volunteering is also a way to learn more about your own strong skills, and perhaps to develop some of your weaker skills and talents which can be parlayed effectively into later job applications. It's a way of exploring whole new avenues of service, self-development, creativity. It's a way to broaden your contact network even before you are ready to job-hunt. And best of all, carefully selected volunteer work can contribute to the welfare of others, allowing you to give of your gifts just a little more to help build the Kingdom.

If you are returning to the job scene after some absence, or if you are preparing to seek your first full-time job, volunteering is an ideal form of preparation. Besides the skill improvement you'll get, the recommendations will be invaluable. And, of course, you're in a box seat to watch the entrances of job openings you may be qualified for right within the organization.

How about it? Is volunteering a way in to something new in your life? Look around.

WORKSHEET 34

1. Where are the career-oriented volunteer opportunities for *you?* Here's a partial list of places that typically use volunteers—with room for you to brainstorm even further.

hospitals	domestic violence	thrift stores
schools	shelters	libraries
day-care centers	chore services	juvenile courts
mental health	departments of	nursing homes
centers	correction	crisis centers
children's homes	senior centers	museums

food banks
non-profit
  agencies
parks/recreation
  centers

churches
community
  theaters
arts organizations
alcohol/drug
  programs

symphony groups
ballets

_____   _____   _____

_____   _____   _____

_____   _____   _____

2. And here's a partial list of volunteer jobs that people do
    in many of these settings. Check any you think you
    might be qualified for.

bookkeeping
reception work,
  phones
sales, promotion
  work
preparing, serving
  meals
supervision
writing, editing
docent services
construction work
recreational
  activities
personal services for elderly or
  handicapped
coordinating recruitment of other
  volunteers

gift shop clerk
scheduling,
  tracking
computer
  programming/
  data entry
mailing list
  maintenance
fund-raising
sewing, mending
tutoring

grant writing
painting
transportation
bulk mailing
graphic arts
publicity work
filing
counseling
carpentry
inventory
  managing

WORKSHEET 35

1. If you think volunteering might help you in your career
    search, match up your talents and skills with some
    places you'd be interested in exploring for volunteer op-
    tions. Make some phone calls. See where they lead.

Skills You Could Offer

a. _____   d. _____

b. _____   e. _____

c. _____   f. _____

Possible Volunteer Targets	*Phone*	*Volunteer Opportunities Here*
a. _____	_____	_____
b. _____	_____	_____
c. _____	_____	_____
d. _____	_____	_____
e. _____	_____	_____

*What You'll Do to Match Available Time/Talents/Skills with a
Volunteer Opportunity:*

_____

_____

_____

_____

Entrepreneuring: Martha's Story

The true spirit of adventure may be your key to the world of employment. Don't rule out the possibility of going into business for yourself.

Granted, some 90 percent of new small businesses fail within a year or two. But what do the 10 percent have that puts them in the winning column? And judging by the sheer number of businesses you see as you drive through most towns in America, there have been a lot of ventures that started someplace, sometime, and made it! So don't say "Mission Impossible."

If you have a special skill, you may be able to showcase it effectively and generate enough demand for your products or services to take care of your needs. Individuals retired or terminated from corporations have often found their know-how vied for in the marketplace, thus becoming successful consultants rather than simply finding another job. Special talent or skill in any field can be marketable. The challenge is to know the talent and its fair market value, identify its market, and bring the two together in the most appealing way possible.

Fresh from a year's sabbatical at an outstanding school of theology, and competent from many years of successful teaching, Martha, a Dominican sister, looked to a new career in education. Her dream was to renew the charism of her congregation through preaching and teaching—not in one school or parish but by traveling throughout the country, from diocese to diocese, wherever people were eager to hear her Good News.

Quality religious education, Martha knew, was at a premium in the smaller towns and rural parishes where resources and finances are often at rock bottom. Her idea was to develop a teaching/preaching team, a solid core of qualified, dedicated persons who could travel with portable equipment and materials, serving the hinterlands with quality adult religious education.

An idea, a fine set of personal qualifications, and a determination! These, together with the blessing of her congregation, constituted all the capital Martha had. But she decided it was enough.

Arriving in her base city, she began her network of contacts. The personal visit, preceded by a letter and a phone call, gave her visibility with every one of the city's pastors, religious education coordinators, diocesan officials, and pastoral ministers. She left attractive, simple brochures, together with overview sheets crisply describing the workshops and courses available. She developed a "keep-in-touch" system with all of them. Martha's personal contacts gave her the local viewpoint on what the people's needs were, and she revised her programs accordingly. She identified time and space problems and developed strategies to counter them. She created a fee schedule with options to make her services affordable to all.

The first year was hard! Martha spent more time on the road promoting than she spent at home. But she got a few commissions, too, and made sure the programs were excellent. She used evaluation comments from participants to spice up her promotional literature.

The hand-to-mouth existence of that first year gave way to increased success in the second, as she responded to requests for her services. Martha counted on the grapevine to help spread the word. And she never let up on her personal contacts: the phone calls, letters, and face-to-face meetings. She strove to learn names and details, and to really "keep in touch."

By the third year, a second Dominican sister asked to join the team, a schedule was established for stops throughout the dioceses, several workshops were coordinated through the diocesan religious education office, and a grant to purchase a van was in the works. Martha was in demand to conduct short retreats, to assist in training parish staffs and religious education teachers, to provide in-service programs for school faculties, ministry groups, and clergy. The two arduous years of seed-planting and friend-making had made the harvest fruitful.

Cottage Industries

Cottage industries are a growing sort of entrepreneuring. You'll find help, if this interests you, through community colleges where convenient workshops and courses teach the basics of operating a business: financing, accounting, marketing, inventory, pricing and fee-setting, advertising, and so on. The Small Business Administration offers literature and services to help a budding Henry Ford get started. Retired executives and managers, some perhaps among your own circle of family and friends, may listen to your ideas and give you tips on what is likely to work and what is doubtful. Check your public library and local bookstores for "how-to" books on starting a business. And don't forget to trust yourself.

Hobbies

Many entrepreneurs have begun as hobbyists. That spare-time skill that relaxes you, renews you, may be your ticket to a lucrative second income and eventually a full-time involvement. Take the group of homemakers in a small Oregon town who parlayed an appliqué sweatshirt project for their church bazaar into a thriving cottage industry. Or the weekend carpenter who got so much work remodeling people's kitchens that he quit his job with a supermarket chain and now employs six workers for "Quality Kitchens, Inc."

Consider creating your own job if you're thinking about change.

WORKSHEET 36

Here are a couple of ads for entrepreneurs getting established on a small scale. After reading them, use your imagination to write your own.

FREELANCE SECRETARY

Special Project? • Overload? • Vacation? • Temporary Vacancy?

Let me help! Personal attention my specialty!

- Business, legal, medical, academic, organizational
- College graduate. I can spell!
- Telephone, machine dictation
- Your office or mine
- Available days, nights, weekends. You name the hours.
- Sense of humor, some genius. Pressure? I thrive on it.

Call me or my answering machine: one of us is always in!
555-9419
Roberta, the Secretary

WINDOWS BY EILEEN

Made-to-order window treatments
from valances to full-draw drapes
Free In-home consultation on fabrics, trims, ideas
Let me help you bring your room to life

Quality and craftsmanship guaranteed
Your recommendation is my bonus

Call for an appointment: 9 A.M.–5 P.M. 928-7179

Now, what skill could you offer to an eager world? Write
your own ad here:

_____

_____

_____

_____

_____

_____

_____

_____

_____

CHAPTER 12

Marketing—Part of the "Call"

Shopping the job market takes all the skills you plan to take with you into that great new job or career. Getting a job, remember, *is* a job! Take it seriously, as a challenge—but not a challenge filled with anxiety and fear. Job search is an objective, practical matter, the common experience of almost every adult person, not once but several times. Take it in stride.

It's good to remember that, even in a reasonably good market, the average job search takes just under four months. In a slow market, it's going to be longer. Remember, too, that you should plan on at least twice as many interviews as you receive job offers, and many times as many applications as interviews achieved. All of this spells time, time you may feel you can't afford if you have separated from a job before having found a new one.

Finally, don't predetermine exactly what this new job or career will be or where it will take you. The Spirit blows where it will. And the one factor you think might be negative *could be* the crown jewel an employer is looking for.

Read Carmelita's and Elise's stories; Carmelita thought she was too old and Elise underestimated her own worth.

Carmelita's Story

With three children, a part-time job, and four senior business classes taking up "twenty-five" hours a day, Carmelita was ready to graduate with an accounting degree. Little sleep over the past few semesters, her guilt over having to snatch hours for family fun, and constant pressure were taking an increasing toll on her as she looked for a job during her last semester. Interviews came and went, and younger graduates grabbed the jobs, until one day Carmelita was a finalist at a small but successful local firm. At her last interview with the company president, Carmelita heard these unbelievable words: "We think you're the candidate we want—you seem willing to stay with us, and you bring maturity." What she thought was her liability—age—was just the asset looked for!

Elise's Story

When she began job-hunting after her three girls were all in school, her only objective was clerical work, what she'd done before marriage. She answered ads and got some interviews, but no job offers. Discouragement was rearing its head when one day, sitting in the reception room at a large, open-concept office, the light went on! Elise realized that, at thirty-six, she was applying for jobs that eighteen-year-olds were doing.

And age wasn't getting them the jobs, inexperience was. She was overqualified. A mature woman with lots to offer to an entry-level position—too much! Employers felt, but never said, that she wouldn't last in the jobs because of boredom.

Elise began looking at other ads, other sources of job

information describing jobs with more responsibility. It was scary, but also an ego boost—looking at herself as more capable, more resourceful, and worth more on the open market! And somebody hired her as just that: more than she had ever dreamed when she hit the job trail.

For two years now, she's been a department supervisor, moving into that position just a year after starting with her new company. She's on line for a special management training program next spring. She can still type and file and do entry-level tasks if needed, but she tries to leave those things for the 18-year-olds. After all, they need the experience!

All these ideas and stories suggest the importance of looking ahead, career-wise. Is there handwriting on the wall? Can you see changes coming, in either the external job environment—reorganization, diversification in the company, new managers, technological changes, graduation from school—or in the inner sense that says a change is becoming increasingly important *for you?*

This is the time to explore, quietly and calmly, the job market around you. It's the time to settle into prayer a little more attentively so the events and feelings of each working day can be integrated into the whole pattern of your life. This may be the time when the Lord can speak most easily in and through those daily events. The call to change is always a call to grow, to become a little more of the whole person whose completion is your life's work.

In this light, exploring the job market is a stronger, more meaningful experience than merely "looking for a job." You have a right to explore the full benefits of this time of searching and discovering. Being able to explore *before* there's a crisis—before you've been laid off, or resigned from your present job—allows you the freedom to proceed effectively in searching out new worlds, as well as to attend peacefully to the daily "nudgings" of God and circumstance.

PART V

What Tools Do You Need? Résumé, Cover Letter, Interview, Follow-Up

You are the light of the world. A city built on a hill-top cannot be hidden. No one lights a lamp to put it under a tub; they put it on a lamp-stand where it shines for everyone in the house. In the same way your light must shine in the sight of all, so that, seeing your good works, they may give praise to your Father in heaven.

Matthew 5:14–16

Tools of the trade, implements, devices, means—whatever you want to call them—do the job of getting you the job! Required by most professions and tailored to provide information quickly and effectively, your résumé, cover letter, application, and thank-you notes are more than pieces of paper or printed forms. These tools facilitate your employment or career change and reflect the fine applicant you are.

Call them steps along the way or tasks to do, but take them seriously and work on them systematically. Start with your résumé and move along the road one step at a time:

RÉSUMÉ   REFERENCES   THANK-YOU LETTER
    ↘   ↗   ↘   ↗
COVER LETTER   INTERVIEW

This section helps plan these important items. Because you need time—hours, days, weeks—start them early so you can ponder, work, and pray.

The exercises in this section will help when you have targeted a job and are actually preparing your résumé, cover letter, and interview. They can also give you an overview of what's to come and some practice in advance of the pressured deadlines.

So with confidence, design the tools to sell the unique and qualified person you are.

CHAPTER 13

Designing a Top Résumé

A résumé is a picture of you, a summary of your experience, skills, and potential. It introduces you to an employer and assists him or her in deciding whether you are a worthy candidate for interviews. Generally, résumés should be tailored to do two things:

- accentuate your qualifications for the position
- meet the needs of the employer

This two-edged focus is difficult, so résumés often tend to be historical, listing the last few years of activity. Although this experience, education, and training are rich parts of your past and help to make you unique, these qualifications are "static" or "what you have done." Your skills and personal qualities, on the other hand, point to the future, are "dynamic," and show "what you can do." Résumés focusing on "will-do" rather than "have-done" spotlight those life experiences and skills that readily transfer into new settings and new opportunities.

P Accentuating Your Potential

aint reality as it has been, but also include a "sales" quality for what will be; in addition to an accurate, concise summary of who you are, create a picture of who you might become. Help your potential employer catch a glimpse of the "self" behind your list of credentials, skills, and work experience.

Then make your data catch the reader's eye. Showing them just what they're looking for lands your résumé on the "Possibly Hire" pile and can result in a call for an interview.

W Format

hat headings should be included, how many details are needed, and what choices do you have? These questions are the big ones—so attack them first. The following pages will help you to make these critical decisions and perhaps even to enjoy yourself along the way.

D Design

oes year-by-year fit you? Or would you rather accent your skills? Or your qualifications? Or what?

Three main designs fit most résumés: the *chronological,* the *functional,* and the *targeted.* Each format has strengths and weaknesses; only after balancing your information, the job you seek, and the impression you wish to make, can you choose the design best suited to your search. But remember, nothing is written in concrete or engraved in gold! Many formats might work. So type out the information you have, rearrange the layout, use transparent tape, and eye it all with an artistic glance. Veterans know that completing a résumé can often take not hours but days.

Samples

For starters, take a peek at the three samples printed here and see what design looks good for you. Check each format —how do the pieces of your life fit into a similar mosaic? Or what parts might you paste together?

Susan M. Kenworth—a fictional friend down the street —wrote a *chronological* sheet to accent her experience through the years, designed a *functional* plan to show her outstanding qualities, and finally *targeted* all her information toward one job. Study these samples and then move on to see strengths and weaknesses of each design.

Chronological Résumé:

SUSAN MARIE KENWORTH

East 7456 Glenrose Drive
Bellingham, Washington
99683

Work Phone:
(304) 345-7890
Message Phone:
(304) 346-8765

EXPERIENCE:

Counselor for Families and the Elderly
   Community Mental Health Clinic
   Othertown, State Zip 1980-1988
    —counseled families and individual members
    —visited adolescents in juvenile detention
    —served on committees for the elderly
    —designed new record system for clients

Homeroom Teacher and Head of Social Science
   Department
   Rural Town High School
   New Town, State Zip 1975-1980
    —taught social studies to senior students
    —directed homeroom activities
    —developed career counseling program
    —moderated student body activities
    —visited the elderly of the community

Junior High School Teacher
   Another Town, State Zip 1970-1975
    —taught eighth-grade homeroom
    —assisted with all-school activities:
    science fair, school paper, sports
    tournaments

EDUCATION: Bachelor of Arts Major: Social
                Studies
                University of My Choice 1970
                Summer Study Major: Counseling
                College of My Choice 1980
                Current State Teacher's Certif-
                icate for Secondary Schools

AFFILIATIONS: State Counseling Associa-
                tion
                County Task Force for Drug
                Abuse

VOLUNTEER WORK:
    Community Mental Health   5 years
    Jail Visiting Program   3 years
    Meals-on-Wheels   2 years
    Study Groups for Migrant Workers 2 years

SPECIAL SKILLS: Organizing office systems
                  for efficient operations
                  Working well on a team

REFERENCES: Available upon request

Functional Résumé:

SUSAN MARIE KENWORTH

East 7456 Glenrose Drive   Work Phone:
Bellingham, Washington   (304) 345-7890
99683   Message Phone:
                                (304) 346-8765

QUALIFICATIONS FOR PARISH MINISTRY:

Organizational Skills

> —designed new filing system for health clinic 550 clients
> —developed career counseling program
> —moderated student body activities in high school 700 students
> —directed homeroom activities in senior and junior high schools

Counseling Skills

> —counseled families and individuals
> —worked with adolescents in Juvenile Detention
> —visited elderly in community

Team Skills

> —served on committees for the elderly
> —worked on study groups for migrant workers
> —worked with counseling team at mental health clinic

EXPERIENCE:

Community Mental Health
Clinic Othertown, State Zip
  Counselor 550 Clients 1980–1988

Rural Town High School   New Town,   State   Zip
   Department Head   700 Student Body   1975-1980

Junior High School   Another Town,   State   Zip
   Teacher/Home Room Advisor   300 Student
   Body   1970-1975

PROFESSIONAL PREPARATION:

Bachelor of Arts Major: Social Studies
   University of My Choice   1970
Summer Study Major: Counseling
   College of My Choice   1980
Current State Teacher's Certificate for Sec-
   ondary Schools

VOLUNTEER WORK:
   Community Mental Health   5 years
   Jail Visiting Program   2 years
   Meals-on-Wheels   2 years
   Study Groups for Migrant Workers   2 years

REFERENCES: Available upon request

Targeted Résumé:

SUSAN MARIE KENWORTH

East 7456 Glenrose Drive   Work Phone:
Bellingham, Washington   (304) 345-7890
99683   Message Phone:
                                   (304) 346-8765

EMPLOYMENT OBJECTIVE:

Assistant Director of Manor Retirement Complex

QUALIFICATIONS:

Organizational Skills
    —designed new filing system for health
     clinic—550 clients
    —developed career counseling program
    —organized activities for high school of
     700 students

Counseling Skills
    —counseled families and individuals
    —worked with adolescents in juvenile detention
    —visited elderly in community

Team Skills
    —served on committees for the elderly
    —worked on study groups for migrant workers
    —worked with counseling team at mental
     health clinic

EXPERIENCE:

COUNSELOR   Community Mental Health Clinic
    Othertown, State Zip 1980-1988

DEPARTMENT HEAD   Rural Town High School
    New Town, State Zip 1975-1980

TEACHER   Junior High School
   Another Town, State Zip 1970-1975

PROFESSIONAL PREPARATIONS:

Bachelor of Arts Major: Social Studies
   University of My Choice 1970
Summer Study Major: Counseling
   College of My Choice 1980

AFFILIATIONS:

State Counseling Association
County Task Force for Drug Abuse

SPECIAL SKILLS: Compassion, Efficiency,
                      Cooperation

VOLUNTEER WORK: Community Mental Health,
                      Jail Visiting Program,
                      Meals-on-Wheels, Study
                      Groups for Migrant Workers

REFERENCES: Furnished upon request

Strengths and Weaknesses

"Sample résumé" is a contradiction in terms just as a "sample person" is hard to find! God has endless variety and no two people fit the same profile. Consequently, one résumé could never fit two individuals, and trying to match a model usually creates problems. Either you try to fit the categories listed and lose some of your uniqueness, or you fail to accent important personal aspects because they seem inconsequential. Watch out for both these traps and emphasize the real individual you are.

Susan Marie Kenworth, our fictional job-seeker, has had experiences not too different from those of hundreds of other people. But her background and activities can be featured in various ways.

Her **chronological** résumé

- lists experience and education, starting with most recent.
- makes affiliations, volunteer work, and special skills accent her teaching and counseling.
- shows her people skills and fine organizational ability as evidence of her high energy and wide interests.

Her **functional** résumé, on the other hand,

- underscores her qualifications.
- simply records her experience over the past thirteen years.
- shows her professional preparation and volunteer work as supporting evidence of her fine qualities.

Her **targeted** résumé

- is closely allied to her functional one in design.
- targets the ONE job sought.
- is usable for this position only.

As you can see, the overall plan of these fundamental designs is the same, and you can choose from a multitude of layouts. Here's an overview of the strengths and weaknesses of each format:

Chronological—gives information in descending order with most recent events listed first under the main headings.

—Effective when
   you have experience in the same profession
   your last position or employer was significant in the field
   your last job shows you have assumed added responsibility

—Not as effective when
   your work history has been diversified
   your previous jobs are not focused toward current goals
   past jobs are similar with little advancement
   your experience is limited

Functional—focuses on skills, aptitudes, and qualities that can be applied to a number of situations.

—Effective when
   you lack specific job-related skills for the new position
   your education is general
   your work experience is considerable and can be put to use immediately

you wish to highlight capabilities and connect many
experiences

—Not as effective when
your job experiences have been similar
your last position or employer would add prestige
you lack competence in broad skill areas

Targeted—presents a specific description of abilities and
achievements with everything directed toward one particular
position.

—Effective when
you wish to *target* a specific job
you are willing to write a new résumé for each position sought
you wish to emphasize how your potential points to
one area

—Not effective when
you wish to use your résumé for many applications
you have no clear career goals
your experience is limited

WORKSHEET 37

1. Which is it! Which will it be for your résumé at this
time? Circle one:

   Chronological   Functional   Targeted

2. What are the advantages of this form for you at this
time?

   _____

   _____

   _____

_____

_____

3. What disadvantages should you be aware of as you
    develop your résumé?

_____

_____

_____

_____

_____

W Mechanics

hat you say on your résumé varies from person to
person and maybe from job to job. But the length, size/
format, printing, and color usually stay within accepted
boundaries. A closer look reveals the logic of these limits:

Length:

- use one sheet; two if work history is exceptional
- being overqualified and/or listing all your experience
  may limit your chances at the job you want, so line
  up all your wonderful qualifications but use selec-
  tively

Size/format:

- use regular 8½-by-11-inch good bond paper; over-
  sized sheets are clumsy and usually end up being
  tossed from the files
- fold carefully; preferably, not at all

Printing:

- choose clear, uncluttered type; beware of intricate designs
- emphasize items with bold type, underlining, different fonts
- have your résumé professionally typed and reproduced; many print shops offer this service for reasonable fees
- be careful not to choose grained paper, which may look elegant but will not reproduce clear copies

Color:

- choose a color that fits you and the job you seek; white is fine; off-white, light grey, beige might set your résumé apart from the crowd
- avoid bright colors and flimsy sheets
- whatever paper you choose, purchase extra matching sheets and envelopes for your cover letter

Aesthetics:

- allow ample margins at top, bottom, and sides
- make "white space" work for you and make items stand out by not crowding your data
- balance your information so your reader sees an attractive page and wants to read all you have to say
- squint at your finished sheet and see whether the right or left side is top-heavy or data is too crowded

Extra Accents

The foregoing suggestions on the mechanics of preparing a résumé should be classified as "generic" and fit most résumés. If, however, you are an artist or a marketing professional, or have special skills you want to show off, then use all the tricks of your trade to fashion a résumé that suits YOU and matches the position you seek. Calligraphy border designs, sketches, and brochure-type formats may fit special professions and enhance or demonstrate your qualifications. However, resort to such embellishments with discretion. For most situations, a precise, professionally written résumé clearly shows how good you are without the extra flourishes!

WORKSHEET 38

1. What do you think is best for *your* résumé:

>   *Length:* Is one page enough? Do you need two? Why?

_____

_____

_____

>   *Size/format:* Are you selling your creativity? If so, do you want an unusual fold, headline format, envelope? Sketch it here!

_____

_____

_____

_____

Printing: What are your options? Which one is your choice?

_____

_____

_____

_____

Color: _____ white

_____ beige

_____ light grey

_____

_____

Which will you choose?

Aesthetics: Anything extra needed: (Remember for "creative" professionals only!)

_____ border design

_____ hand-drawn lines

_____ calligraphy

_____

2. What information do you need before you can decide about these factors? Check them off and put on your TO DO list.

_____ Should you go to a print shop and see some samples?

_____ Should you go to the library and study some examples?

_____ Whom do you know in your neighborhood, family, work that could help?

_____ Other?

3. Right now you need to get information on

_____

_____

_____

_____

Items to Include

Most résumés include basic information:

1. Identification
2. Main subject headings
3. Experience
4. Education
5. Awards and Honors
6. Special Skills
7. Affiliations (professional and volunteer)
8. Interests and activities, if pertinent
9. Other

Taking one section at a time will help. Throw out what doesn't fit you and add choice items that pop up along the way. Keep your goal in mind and move along step by step. Ready?

A Good Start

Identification

You deserve top billing so begin with your name. Never put "Résumé" atop the page! You usually don't write the word "Letter" above your correspondence to tell what it is. "Résumé" is equally redundant. Make your name appear prominent both now and three weeks down the road when they pull your carefully planned résumé from the file for a second look.

Put your name where you think it looks best. Center it and use capitals like this:

SUSAN MARIE KENWORTH

or underline it like this:

Susan Marie Kenworth

or do both like this:

SUSAN MARIE KENWORTH

When your name is centered, underlined, and surrounded with white space, even the quickest scan will not miss it.

Or perhaps you prefer the off-center look. If so, try this, flush left:

SUSAN MARIE KENWORTH

Be careful, however, so that additional details don't add confusion.

Address and Phone Numbers

Likewise, your address and phone number or numbers must be clearly and quickly accessible. Using ample space, and carefully planning these important elements, will add to the crisp, professional sheet you want. Many employers phone candidates during regular business hours, so listing a message phone—either an answering machine or a family member or roommate—can prevent your missing that important call. Caution, however! Give your message-taker explicit directions—you want no potential employer to know you are taking a nap, even though you have been up all night writing résumés. Remember that even the fondest of grandmothers and the best of friends often have the disarming ability to reveal some fact that you prefer kept private.

The following arrangement gives your information clearly and quickly:

SUSAN MARIE KENWORTH

East 7456 Glenrose Drive
Bellingham, Washington 99683

Work Phone: (304) 345-7890
Message Phone: (304) 346-8765

You may wish to save space and utilize the side margins like this:

SUSAN MARIE KENWORTH

East 7456 Glenrose Drive   Work Phone:
Bellingham, Washington   (304) 345-7890
99683   Message Phone:
                                  (304) 346-8765

Or, preferring the off-center style, you might choose this:

SUSAN MARIE KENWORTH

East 7456 Glenrose Drive,
Bellingham, Washington 99683
Work: (304) 345-7890
Message: (304) 346-8765

Some employment specialists maintain that these details should appear at the end of your résumé, arguing that your qualifications and experience, your skills and interests are more important than a static address and telephone number. Others say this information should be easy to find—at the top. You choose!

Notice, however, that *nothing* is abbreviated; résumés are formal documents and every detail should reflect that focus.

WORKSHEET 39

Which format for identification do you choose?

_____

_____

_____

_____

What are the advantages of this format?

_____

_____

_____

_____

What might be disadvantages?

_____

_____

Main Subject Headings

Your experience, training, education, affiliations, honors, interests, and activities (how's that for a list?) should be ranked according to importance. That's easier said than done. What you think is important *is* important, but what the employer thinks is important must be considered, too. Your arrangement depends on what you wish to convey.

Overall Picture

Do you hope to spotlight your recent computer training, or do you wish to emphasize your long involvement in successful health care? Do you wish to point out the qualities that have been effective in all your past positions? Or do you, as a new graduate, wish to accent your up-to-date training? Busy employers quickly glance over résumés, seeking the key qualifications they need. Knowing the job and knowing yourself permits you to match the two, and dictates what to put first.

WORKSHEET 40

1. From this list of possible subject headings, check off those you might use:

    _____ Education

    _____ Experience

    _____ Leadership

    _____ Activities

    _____ Honors

_____ Awards

_____ Volunteer Activity

2. Or would headings that highlight your qualifications suit you better?

_____ Related Skills and Qualifications

_____ Sales and Customer Relations

_____ Leadership in Civic Community

_____ Volunteer Activities/Church and Civic

_____ Capabilities

_____ Achievements

_____ Selected Educational Training

_____ Committee Membership/Leadership

_____ Programs Designed/Implemented

_____

_____

_____

_____

3. Now arrange these headings to accent your best qualifications. If years of successful work experience best prepare you for your next position, put this information first. Church or civic involvement might be your second outstanding item, and volunteer activities may rate third place. If education is your top qualification, give it a position accenting its importance.

Your Picture

Decide what best suits the job you seek from among all the skills and qualities you offer. Then do the following worksheet.

WORKSHEET 41

1. If you're applying for _____, you think the best headings to use will include these:

Your Headings	Why You'll Use Them
a. _____	a. _____
b. _____	b. _____
c. _____	c. _____
d. _____	d. _____
e. _____	e. _____

2. Right now, you think it best not to include the following headings but you want to remember them for future jobs:

a. _____

b. _____

c. _____

d. _____

Focusing Your Work History

Choosing your subject headings moves you along the road, so keep trudging on! Now decide what details you need to round out your qualifications. Options abound! Again, take one step at a time. Start with your experience. It speaks loud and clear: YOU ARE QUALIFIED AND READY and YOU HAVE FAITH IN YOUR FUTURE!

Where You Worked

Do you wish to accent *where* you worked, *what role* you had, or your *qualifications?* What's your answer? Be brave—indicate your choice here and come back to reconsider it later.

What's your best option? Circle it.

WHERE   WHAT   QUALIFICATIONS

If you worked somewhere especially significant—parish, school, or institution—you probably would highlight the *where*. But this decision can be tricky. Perhaps one place was significant but the other three were not. Trade-offs are the answer, but be consistent. If you highlight the *where* for one place, all the other experiences listed should accent the *where*, too.

Here are several examples with the *where* emphasized. Do they give you an idea?

CENTRAL CITY HIGH SCHOOL   1,800 students
    Maintown,   State   Zip   Code
    Department Head and Mathematics Teacher

FAMILY MENTAL HEALTH CLINIC
    Othertown,   State   Zip   Code
    Office Supervisor

WORKSHEET 42

1. Now line up your experience and accent *where* you worked. Ready? Start by putting down the

    PLACE: _____

        City and State: _____

        Your Title: _____

Now, do it again for the next job.

PLACE: _____

    City and State: _____

    Title: _____

And again; make it look like this all the way through.

PLACE: _____

    City and State: _____

    Title: _____

What Your Role Was

Your role might be more important than the place you worked; if so, put it first and put the institution in a less conspicuous place. Here are the same experiences with *what role* you played emphasized. Do you like this better?

DEPARTMENT HEAD and MATHEMATICS TEACHER
    Central City High School   1,800 students
    Maintown,   State   Zip   Code

OFFICE SUPERVISOR
    Family Mental Health Clinic
    Othertown,   State   Zip   Code

WORKSHEET 43

1.   Now do the same, listing first in bold words *what role* you played, and give *where* you worked less emphasis.

    WHAT (your title or your role): _____

    Place: _____

    Address: _____

WHAT: _____

Place: _____

Address: _____

WHAT: _____

Place: _____

Address: _____

WHAT: _____

Place: _____

Address: _____

And list all your important jobs just to be sure you have them on record here—whether you use them all in this résumé or not.

What Your Qualifications Are

Maybe you ought to de-emphasize the roles and the places you have worked. By pointing out your qualities and significant achievements you may paint a better picture of the real you. In this case, the following format might be preferable. Try listing your qualifications under one or two headings and then put where you worked in a subsequent section. Here's how it might look:

COMMUNICATION SKILLS:
    —edited monthly newsletter with circulation of 2,000
    —was secretary to three lawyers and wrote all executive minutes
    —speak extemporaneously with ease

ORGANIZATIONAL SKILLS:
    —managed time effectively while earning a 3.4 GPA

in college and working 20 hours a week at an outside job
—handled variety of tasks in a large office
—worked under pressure to meet deadlines without
sacrificing quality of work

The same person with the same skills! But new designs
bring new accents.

WORKSHEET 44

1. What verbs could you use to underscore your skills and
    qualifications? (See Appendix, page 261 for a list of
    strong, active verbs.)

    • _____ • _____ • _____

    • _____ • _____ • _____

2. When it comes to SKILLS, you could write that you

    • _____

    • _____

    • _____

    • _____

3. And when it comes to QUALIFICATIONS, you could
    say that you are able to

    • _____

    • _____

    • _____

    • _____

Common Sense

Planning the experience section of your résumé is probably the most difficult part of the process. Choosing the data and the format demands careful thought, and no one way is best. Begin with your most recent experience unless you have a good reason to do otherwise. And then let your common sense guide you. Be sure that your data lends credence to your qualifications. Using the title "Selected Experiences" allows you to choose the most recent ones. Try not to leave gaps in the chronology.

Choosing the Details

With the main experiences listed, decide what details, if any, you will use to prove your competence. A teacher or office supervisor, for example, has many skills often taken for granted; thus it may be advisable to highlight or summarize your own skills, or to create your own format.

Highlight Specific Duties

When presented effectively, even ordinary skills tell a lot about what you can do for the new employer. Some ways to spotlight them and describe their positive results are shown here.

Department Head and Mathematics Teacher
—headed math curriculum committee for five years
—changed math department procedure to meet needs of gifted and remedial students
—supported beginning teachers—all three stayed to become fine additions to staff

—started county Math Fair to encourage students in
this field

Office Supervisor
    —trained two assistants
    —wrote policy for smooth office operations
    —organized system for filing patients' data
    —cut budget expenses by 10% over a two-year period

If you choose this format and have your résumé professionally typed, ask the printer for different types of "bullets"
—such as asterisks (*) or crosses (+)—to accent your lists.
Beware of fancy marks that draw attention to themselves
rather than to your data!

Summarize Specific Duties

You may prefer to write out your duties or responsibilities; this plan can be effective, as shown here.

Department Head and Mathematics Teacher

Duties included: heading math curriculum committee
for five years; changing math department procedure
to meet needs of gifted and remedial students;
supporting beginning teachers—all three stayed to
become fine additions to staff; starting county Math
Fair to encourage students in this field.

Office Supervisor

Trained two assistants; wrote policy for smooth office
operations; organized system for filing patients' data;
cut budget expenses by 10% over a two-year period.

Other formats work equally well. Choose one to enhance your particular qualifications and to help your reader quickly find your key skills.

WORKSHEET 45

1. These specifics will best describe and spotlight your background:

    a. _____

    b. _____

    c. _____

    d. _____

    e. _____

    f. _____

    g. _____

2. Take one of your former experiences and decide which way—by highlighting or summarizing—you'll best display the specific tasks involved. Do that here:

    _____

    _____

    _____

Other Headings

With your experience detailed and ready to be committed to print, move to the other qualifications you listed as top priorities. Take each one and decide what information an employer might want to know. Some general ideas follow:

Education

Degrees are important; dates of acquiring them may not be. Listing individual courses may be appropriate, especially when they point to your potential new job. Summer school classes, seminars, workshops, and other such short-term activities can go under titles like "Additional Study" or "Selected Upgrading." Or create your own specific headline!

WORKSHEET 46

1. Scribble down all the lectures, workshops, seminars you've sat through during the past few years, such as the following:

   • Parent-Teacher lectures
   • church adult education programs
   • neighborhood presentations on Block Watch or environmental problems
   • _____
   • _____
   • _____
   • _____

Maybe these activities didn't result in a degree, but they've added to your experience and background. Keep them on tap; they may come in handy later, during interviews.

2. Now jot down whatever degrees or certificates you might have, night classes you've taken, and any other pertinent educational information.

   a. _____
   b. _____

c. _____

d. _____

Choose the educational data that fits you and the job you seek!

Awards

Write out full titles of awards and sponsoring agencies. If you've been Scout Mom of the Year or Best Volunteer to the Elderly, that shiny plaque highlights a remarkable achievement. Although you are familiar with your own successes and are tempted to say, "It's nothing," others should be made to recognize the wonderful and capable person you are.

WORKSHEET 47

1. Your awards include:

    a. _____

    b. _____

    c. _____

2. Just for fun, write the title of the awards you know you deserve and the ones God will give you someday! For starters, you might include things like these:

    - best spaghetti cook in the parish
    - top babysitter in the whole family
    - foremost seller of raffle tickets
    - greatest coach of school volleyball team

    - _____
    - _____
    - _____

- _____
- _____

(If you need an extra sheet to list them all, go to it!)

Honors

This category is similar to the one you just finished, and deserves the same attention. These recognitions may be especially pertinent if they indicate your success or continued development in a particular area, or if they complement the job you seek. Debating honors in high school, and belonging to Toastmasters International for the past six years, both reinforce your competence in public speaking. On the other hand, winning the poster contest in junior high probably has no significance on your résumé today!

But pondering all those honors and achievements received and those earned but still to be acknowledged gives you time to remember many of those experiences you listed in Chapter 1.

WORKSHEET 48

1. List those you intend to include on your résumé now, AND those that will be there someday!

    RIGHT NOW, you'll include:

    a. _____

    _____

    b. _____

    _____

    c. _____

    _____

SOMEDAY, you'll add:

a. _____

_____

b. _____

_____

c. _____

_____

Special Skills:

Your ability to organize, work under pressure, adapt, or be accurate with numbers may set you apart. Computer knowledge and other technological training are often sought by employers. One applicant had a chauffeur's license and listed it on her résumé under Special Skills when applying for a job as Coordinator of Senior Citizen Activities. Well-qualified, she got the position and drove the chartered bus for many a senior picnic and sightseeing tour. What kind of bus can you drive?

WORKSHEET 49

1. What are your special skills that are particularly pertinent to the job you're seeking?

- organizing volunteers
- working under pressure
- typing 80 words a minute
- writing grants
- operating a word processor
- developing a budget

- _____

- _____

Affiliations—Professional and Volunteer

This category can help to point out your willingness to serve others, your talent for teamwork, and your interest in the community. Although helping others is integral to your Christian life, recalling all the ways the Lord lets you serve can be an energizing assignment. Try it.

WORKSHEET 50

1. Volunteer work you've done for

- your neighborhood

   _____

   _____

- your family

   _____

   _____

- your church

   _____

   _____

- your civic community

   _____

   _____

- other

   _____

   _____

2. Affiliations you maintain include these:

    • Church/Religious

    _____

    _____

    • Charitable

    _____

    _____

    • Civic/Political

    _____

    _____

    • Cultural/Environmental/Social Action

    _____

    _____

    • Other

    _____

    _____

Interests and Activities

These enterprises may or may not be relevant. Hobbies and leisure-time activities may reflect a well-rounded individual who offsets a desk job with athletic interests, or one who enjoys classical music after a day on the road. What about you?

Detailed listings of such items may also erroneously show you as one who dabbles and has little stability; listing seven leisure-time activities is worse than imprudent!

Again, what focuses attention upon the special you?

WORKSHEET 51

1. Choose one:

_____ 1. Your hobbies and interests have no relevance to your career change at this time.

_____ 2. Your hobbies and interests are relevant, and you will list these:

a. _____

_____

b. _____

_____

c. _____

_____

Further Details

Few résumés today include personal statistics. Being six feet tall, slim, or married has little to do with most jobs. Many states prohibit employers from asking questions that are not job-related; be circumspect.

Some items present special problems and demands, and you must work with these. Institutional names that are long, cities and states that require twenty or more spaces, complex experience involving different time spans—all these constraints require singular and, sometimes, difficult planning on your part. Again, using scissors and paste—arranging and fashioning different plans—takes ingenuity and persistence. But the time is well worth it when you eventually own a résumé that reflects not only your life experiences and qualifications, but also your uniqueness.

Another Option

The Information Letter

Perhaps an information letter that skips the formality of the printed résumé suits you better. It can offer your important data more casually and may even elicit an answer.

Job-seekers sometimes send out these carefully crafted letters in place of the cover letter and résumé. If employers like what you offer in this friendly manner, they will respond and request your formal document.

The information letter is not necessarily a substitute for your résumé, but a more informal way of first contacting prospective employers.

Study the following sample letter and see if it fits your needs better than the typical chronological, functional, and targeted plan.

Sample

Your Address
Your Town, State Zip
Date

Employer's Name and Title
Company
City, State Zip

Dear _____:

Nancy Endicott of your _____ Department encouraged me to apply for your position of _____. My accomplishments show I could assist you, and include the following:

- As director of the Counseling Center in _____, I (list your accomplishments in positive and active terms).
- As supervisor of _____ at _____, I (list your accomplishments in this job).
- At _____ Company, I worked as _____ and accomplished (list your accomplishments).

My formal education includes a Bachelor of Arts in Counseling from _____ University and night classes at _____ during the past four years. I will be happy to provide a full résumé if you wish.

Next week I will call your office to set up an appointment that is convenient for you when we can meet to discuss further Company X and my qualifications. I look forward to talking with you.

Sincerely,

Your Handwritten Name

Your Typed Name

1. What do you think about an informational letter?

_____

_____

_____

2. Why?

_____

_____

_____

_____

Final Tips

Final tips for a successful résumé include these:

- Use action words—a list is included in the Appendix on page 261.
- Design your data for easy skimming so key items stand out.
- Avoid cluttering the page with dates—tuck them behind and beneath more important information—and use only if necessary.
- Give examples to show accomplishments whenever possible.
- Rarely, if ever, use personal pronouns. (Say "Directed sales, updated inventory, trained new employees" rather than "I directed sales, I updated, etc.")
- Avoid all slang, contractions, and "buzz" words.
- Proofread and eliminate all errors.
- Reproduce copies professionally—never send a faint or dirty copy.
- Show a draft of your résumé to other professionals and friends for their reactions.

- Keep a copy of all final drafts for future reference.
- Tailor separate résumés to fit the different jobs you seek.

Make It YOU

Whether you underline, use a bold typeface, indent, write descriptions, or list key points—the overall picture is most important. Make your résumé summarize you—your past and your present, your strengths and your potential.

Like all important documents, résumés need consultation. So heed the advice given to writers that says, "Never fall in love with your first draft!" Ask a friend, colleague, or co-worker to study yours, and then listen to their suggestions. Know that every person, however, will have only his or her opinion of what is best. The final choice is yours alone—the résumé is you!

But have fun—enjoy the recalling and the planning—and revel in the rich and incredible person you are.

CHAPTER 14

Writing a Cover or Application Letter

As a combination, your application letter and résumé show you have the qualifications, experience, and energy to fill the position. Together, these documents communicate who you are and what you want.

Your cover letter introduces you to your potential employer and gives that first glimpse of you as an employee. It must

- catch attention,
- set you apart from dozens of applicants, and
- make looking at your résumé seem worthwhile.

Tailored to fit just ONE basic situation and carefully designed to entice, it invites further investigation of your qualifications.

How you think and organize; how you spell, punctuate, and write; how you present yourself as a professional; and how you will benefit your employer—all these qualities shine through from your simple application letter.

Guidelines

How much data you include and how you arrange it depend on circumstances, but here are a few general suggestions:

1. Show that you know how to write a good business letter. See page 197 for an acceptable form.

2. Address your letter to a specific person. If you do not know who will be hiring, telephone to find out. Ask for the name, and title, if any. Correct spelling is essential. Few personnel directors wish to be known as "To Whom It May Concern." A phone call for the needed information helps you personalize your letter—even if it must be a long distance call. And doing this bit of research shows that you care enough to check details. If, however, the newspaper advertisement you are responding to gives instructions to write to "Department T," write to Department T!

3. Type your letter on bond paper or something that matches your résumé. White, grey, beige, and ivory are suitable.

4. Tailor every cover letter to the individual company. *Never* send a photocopied "form" letter. It is acceptable, however, to generate your letter from a word processor if the printer produces sufficiently dark and high quality type. Perhaps now is the time to put in a new ribbon.

5. Fold your letter properly and use a legal-size envelope. Or better still, send letter and résumé in a flat manila envelope. Make every effort to insure that

your documents arrive looking crisp and professional.

6. If you are asking for information, include a self-addressed, stamped envelope for convenient return.

7. Keep a file copy of every letter you send.

K Length

Keep your letter BRIEF. Accent key ideas and help your reader quickly grasp your message. Save intricate details for the interview. Some general tips include:

1. Show how you can benefit your employer.

2. Highlight key strengths that fit the position.

3. Slant your ideas toward the future.

4. Include qualities that make you stand out: quick learner, organized, persuasive, flexible, work well under pressure.

5. Call attention to your enclosed résumé and one or two key items listed therein.

B Planning

Before getting lost in the details, sit back, relax, and think for a minute. Then try this process to clarify where you want your letter to go and how to make it say what you want. Answer the WHY? WHAT? and HOW? questions that follow.

WORKSHEET 52

1. *Why* are you writing this letter? Pinpoint the reasons. If you are vague about this task, your reader will be even more confused.

    You are writing this letter in order to

    _____

    _____

    _____

2. *What* do you want to say? If you picked up the telephone and had just sixty seconds to say, "Please hire me because . . ."—WHAT would you say? Quickly jot down these ideas in random order. Keep listing until there are at least ten.

    Hire me because

    a. _____

    b. _____

    c. _____

    d. _____

    e. _____

    f. _____

    g. _____

h. _____

i. _____

j. _____

3. *How* do you arrange these key ideas for the strongest impact? Study the ten reasons just listed and then list the top five:

   a. _____

   b. _____

   c. _____

   d. _____

   e. _____

Now that you have your WHY, WHAT, and HOW, relax again and talk it over with yourself. Tell *why* you want the position and *what* you have to offer. Say it again—and again. Picture your potential employer intently listening to you as you explain and entice.

With this skeletal outline, you are ready to draft each part of your letter: opening, middle, and ending. But before writing, study the following descriptions of the three main sections and what each one can do.

Arranging the Data

Good business letters have powerful openings and closings. So, too, has a good application letter. Gain ATTENTION in the beginning and elicit ACTION in the close, and use brief paragraphs (two or three sentences) summarizing your key attributes in the middle.

Attention in the Opening

1. Write something uniquely associated with the person, position, or institution you are addressing to show that you are communicating personally.

2. Try, if possible, to name the job and why you are qualified.

3. Rarely, if ever, write "This is to apply for . . ." Rather, catch the reader's attention with some pertinent data.

4. Tell how you know about the position; if possible, name someone who could lend status to your credentials.

Perhaps these opening sentences suit your case:

a. Your position for a tutor in the Pediatrics Department matches my wide experience as a teacher. Working with kindergarten and first grade children, and coordinating school activities, have prepared me to set up your program and to work with parents of your preschool patients.

b. Jane Smith [be sure she is in good standing!] on your Board encouraged me to seek your position for an executive secretary. Both my qualifications and experience match your needs.

c. After studying your [company, school, parish, hospital, etc.], I believe my experience of [   ] will suit your needs.

Key Points in the Body

Answer a few more questions and you will have all the important items for the middle paragraphs.

1. What do you think the employer wants?
2. What do you have to offer?
3. How can you match the two?
4. What will you spotlight?
5. What one or two items from your résumé will you note in your letter without repeating the résumé?
6. How will you show that your skills can transfer if your experience does not directly fit the job you now seek?

WORKSHEET 53

1. What specifics from your résumé will you include in your middle paragraphs?

- _____
- _____
- _____
- _____

Action in the Closing

More questions can help to clarify what should be in your final paragraph:

1. What do you want to happen next?
2. Do you wish more information or the job description?
3. Will you call for an appointment?
4. Will you stop by to pick up a brochure?

Whatever you decide, let the reader know what action will be taken. Make your intentions fit the situation, and make them simple and definite:

1. "I will call next week to make an appointment convenient for you" shows initiative and follow-through.
2. "The recommendations you request will be forwarded this week" shows you have followed directions given in the advertisement.
3. "I look forward to talking with you about [your new project, the plans you have for this position, or whatever is pertinent]" personalizes your letter to this one situation.

Numbers 1 and 2 may fit your letter; numbers 1 and 3 may be preferable. Or mix and match to give it that final zip and demonstrate your interest in the position you seek.

Fitting It All Together

Sample

Here is a sample letter sent to St. Henry's Parish; it offers you an example of what others write in that not-so-formidable application letter.

```
1234 Front Street
Anywhere You Want
June 6, 19-

Joan Werning, President
St. Henry's Pastoral Council
City, State Zip

Dear Joan Werning:

Your opening for a coordinator of Volunteers
for the Elderly at St. Henry's Parish matches
my training and my experience. Mr. Joe Smith
of your Pastoral Council encouraged me to
apply for this position.

    With a degree in Social Work and many years
as an administrator, I have developed a
compassion and admiration for the elderly and
an effective management style.

    Please note on the enclosed résumé my
leadership achievements and my volunteer work
in several parishes. Also, my dedication,
flexibility, and sense of humor seem to suit
this special ministry.

    Early next week, I will call to confirm the
arrival of this application and ask for an
appointment convenient to you. If you need
further information before we meet, I can be
```

reached at (509) 326-3436 between 8:00 A.M.
and 5:00 P.M.

   I look forward to talking with you about the
fine program Joe Smith has described at St.
Henry's.

Sincerely,

Your Handwritten Name

Your Typed Name

Generic Letter

Here is a generic letter. Use it as an outline or guide, but make your letter YOUR letter!

```
Your Present Address
City, State Zip
Date of Writing

Name
Title
Company, Institution, or Parish
City, State Zip

Dear _____ :
```

1st Paragraph: Use your first sentence to name the position and your general qualifications. Say how you heard about the position or who told you (if this person is well thought of). Use this first paragraph to give essential data and to catch attention.

2nd Paragraph: Highlight one or two of your top qualities. Take the employer's viewpoint —tell how you can help, fit the need, or bring special training. Let employer know you are interested in the company or location.

3rd Paragraph: Refer to your enclosed résumé or application form and note one or two important items.

4th Paragraph: Take the initiative: you will stop by, you will call, etc. Do not expect your reader to contact you. If you wish more information, include a stamped envelope. In closing, make sure your reader knows what follow-through is expected on both sides.

Sincerely yours,

Your Handwritten Name

Your Typed Name

WORKSHEET 54

1. Write your own cover letter here. When finished, go back and check your draft against the model on page 195.

   Opening Paragraph: _____

   _____

   _____

   _____

   Middle Paragraphs: _____

   _____

   _____

   _____

   Closing Paragraph: _____

   _____

   _____

   _____

CHAPTER 15

Preparing a Winning Interview

Interviews come in assorted sizes and shapes, and experts disagree on the fundamentals and the frills. These all-important meetings can be as casual as conversations with a friend, or as formal as facing a team of experts taking turns quizzing you. They can be the result of networking—of "someone knowing someone who knows someone"—or the result of three months of concerted effort in a methodical search. But most interviews have some common characteristics. They

- are an exchange of ideas
- allow interviewer and interviewee to give and receive information
- should benefit both parties
- can be short or long
- can include an interviewer or a team
- involve personalities

- should be positive experiences
- are usually the last step before employment
- demand careful planning

Power

Whether your interview is casual or formal, whether it is with one person or a team, whether it is your first or fiftieth, you have the power to make it successful. Your positive attitude toward it requires the following:

1. Remember that your interview is a conversation and *you* have control over your attitude, what you say, your appearance, and the questions you ask.

2. Realize you cannot control the place, the pace, the interviewer, or the questions he or she asks.

3. Know what information you want to give and to get.

4. Know that you are competent and will do your best.

5. Realize that not being offered the position is a refusal, but not a rejection of you as a person.

Key Factors

Although experts, manuals, and mentors differ on the rules for an interview, the three main steps of *planning, practicing,* and *presenting* get to the heart of your challenge. And these three steps include seven key factors.

1. Why Do You Want This Job?
2. What Is the "Big Picture"?
3. What Job Skills Do You Have?

4. What Personal Qualities and Human Relations Traits Do You Have to Offer?

5. What Questions Should You Prepare to Answer?

6. What Questions Should You Ask?

7. How Do You Open and Close the Interview?

Why Do You Want This Job?

If you do not know exactly why you want this job, you risk being indefinite in your goals, in articulating your qualifications, and in convincing an employer that you are the best candidate. So, start by analyzing the "WHY".

The following exercise will help you prepare for a specific interview; or perhaps you prefer to dream a little and use it to plan for your ideal job.

WORKSHEET 55

1. You want this job

   because _____

   because _____

   because _____

2. It will meet your need

   to _____

   to _____

   to _____

3. You can live out your values

    of _____

    of _____

    of _____

4. You can assist your employer

    by _____

    by _____

    by _____

What Is the Big Picture?

Some facts and figures can be obtained only in the interview, but be sure that you know the "big picture" before walking through the door and shaking hands. When a recent college graduate was asked in an interview what he knew of the company, he replied, "I know you make good refrigerators." The interviewer coldly replied, "We haven't manufactured refrigerators for ten years!" Needless to say, the applicant did not have the picture or get the job.

So find out the general facts. A few samples follow:

Office Job   —What products or services are provided?
                 —What is the organizational structure of
                    the office?
                 —Who is the supervisor?
                 —With whom would you be working?

Store   —Is it locally or nationally owned?
                 —Who are the competitors?
                 —What is the financial picture?

Social Service   —Is there local, state, or federal funding?
                 —Is it privately owned?
                 —What programs are offered?
                 —What services are provided?

Hospital   —Who owns it: private, county, etc.?
                 —What specialties?
                 —What philosophy?

Hotel   —Is it local or chain-operated?
                 —How many rooms?
                 —Are there special services?
                 —What is the structure of authority?

WORKSHEET 56

As practice in getting the big picture, develop some questions you might research on the following possible places of employment:

Church _____

_____

_____

Restaurant _____

_____

_____

School or University _____

_____

_____

Your Job Skills

Because you cannot tell an interviewer *all* your skills or experience, you should choose those that are most important and describe how you effectively used them. Have these little scenarios ready to slip into that crucial half-hour no matter what formal questions are asked.

If possible, tell the effects of your skills:

- You planned a new procedure and it saved five hours a week.
- Your ability to work with people made you successful in promoting a management team.
- Your ability to organize put the fund-raising campaign over the goal.
- Your computer skills allowed you to keep up with the pressure of daily demands.

WORKSHEET 57

What are your scenarios—those important items illustrating your effectiveness that you must weave into your interview? And what concrete details will you give to support your point?

1. Skill: _____

   Details you will give to prove: _____

   _____

2. Skill: _____

    Details: _____

    _____

    _____

3. Skill: _____

    Details: _____

    _____

    _____

4. Skill: _____

    Details: _____

    _____

    _____

Personal Qualities and "Human Relations" Traits

Although skills and special training are important when you seek employment, personal qualities also play an essential role. They reflect the rich person you are.

WORKSHEET 58

1. Every employer seeks these work qualities. Check the ones you have to offer:

    dedication   ability to follow
                                      directions

loyalty	willingness to work overtime
commitment to working hard	affability
flexibility	generosity
responsibility	efficiency
good nature	fairness
energy	honesty
creativity	neatness
prudence	optimism
punctuality	enthusiasm

2. Choose three or four of your best qualities and jot down what you do to demonstrate them:

    Quality   How You Demonstrate It

    a. _____   _____

    b. _____   _____

    c. _____   _____

3. "Human relations" traits also set you apart and reflect that Christian reverence you have for all people. Sensitive to others, sensing their uniqueness, you are (check off what applies):

courteous	pleasant
cheerful	reconciling
listening	gentle
understanding	obliging
tactful	friendly
respectful	grateful
helpful	kind
personable	supportive

4. Human relations traits you confidently possess are:

Trait	When You've Demonstrated This Trait
a. _____	_____
b. _____	_____
c. _____	_____
d. _____	_____

Questions to Prepare

The two basic questions about you in the mind of your potential employer are:

WHY SHOULD I HIRE YOU? WHY DO YOU WANT
TO WORK HERE?

Having analyzed the big picture, and ascertained your own skills, qualities, and values, you are ready! You know the facts about the employer and can give concrete examples of your competence, relating them to the job you seek.

Books, tapes, workshops abound telling you what specific questions to prepare. But no one knows for sure. One applicant had "fly fishing" listed as an interest on her résumé, and her interviewer was an avid fisherman. The first ten minutes were spent on how to tie the flies and where to go for the best trout!

However, here are some good queries frequently encountered:

1. Tell me about yourself.
2. Why do you wish to work here?
3. Why are you leaving your present job?
4. What are your long-range goals? Short-range?

5. What is important to you in a job?

6. What are your strengths? Weaknesses?

7. What accomplishments are you most proud of?

8. What gives you satisfaction?

9. Would you call yourself a team worker? Explain.

10. Do you seek and accept responsibility? Can you give an example?

11. How do others describe you?

12. What is the most difficult assignment you ever had? What did you learn?

13. What is the most rewarding assignment you ever had? Why?

14. What qualities do you bring to this job? How can they help us?

15. How do you take criticism? Give an example.

16. Are you self-motivated? Give an example.

17. Why should we hire you?

18. What interests and hobbies do you have?

19. Describe the qualities you seek in a supervisor.

20. Have you ever had authority? How did you use it?

21. What ideas would you like to implement with us?

22. Do you have any doubts about this job?

23. What unique qualities would you bring to it?

24. How long do you plan to stay?

25. What salary do you expect?

WORKSHEET 59

1. Play-act an interview and answer five of the preceding questions right now. Be an interviewer and look yourself straight in the eye!

Question #1: _____

Answer _____

Question #2: _____

Answer _____

Question #3: _____

Answer _____

Question #4: _____

Answer _____

Question #5: _____

Answer _____

2. Where did you show your stuff? What questions did you answer like an expert?

    a. _____
    b. _____
    c. _____

3. What questions did you hedge, stutter, "um and ah" over? Be honest.

    a. _____
    b. _____
    c. _____

4.   Here's your practice plan—choose one or two or three ways to prepare:

_____ Ask a friend to conduct a mock interview.

_____ Tape-record your answers; re-do the difficult ones three times and choose the best.

_____ Type questions on 3×5 cards and practice answering them while waiting for a bus or a dental appointment.

"Hidden" Questions

Some of these questions can be tricky, and many have hidden agendas:

1.   "What is important to you in a job?" might be intended to find out whether your values fit the workplace, and/or whether you are stable, hard-working, and willing to learn.

2.   "What are your goals?" may be intended to reveal your self-knowledge and degree of reflection.

3.   "Do you seek responsibility?" could be a measure of your energy.

Probably the hardest questions might be about your weaknesses. If you have none, you're not real; and if you have too many, you're not wanted! So name a weakness of yours that you have strengthened, and explain what the positive effects of that are today. For example:

"Because I have high energy, I used to plan too many things in one day or one week. With better time management now, I still get lots done but am more realistic."

Or if this is too idealistic, try this:

"My quiet ways, which I once saw as a weakness, are turning into a strong asset. I am working with a volunteer group that needs someone to listen and help with problem-solving, and I have become an effective ombudsman."

Whatever your answer, turn a past negative into a future positive. Plan how to describe your less-than-perfect humanity. This planning is particularly important if you have been terminated from a previous position, and a weakness in your performance might thus be noted.

WORKSHEET 60

1. A weakness you might suggest is _____

_____

2. You'll turn it into a positive by _____

_____

Compensation

Salary, too, is difficult to discuss, so be prepared. It can be listed in the job description, discussed when the position is offered, or mentioned when a compromise on benefits is being reached. Know the average salary range in your geographical area for the job you want, and be able to give a quote if directly asked. Giving an amount in the upper range allows you to negotiate, and avoids beginning lower than the employer had expected. You might also ask, "What salary range and benefits do you offer here?" And then with your research in mind, your next response comes naturally.

Because salary and benefits are peculiar to individual situations, probably the only general rule that can be proclaimed is that this question is never the first one you ask.

WORKSHEET 61

Check off the ways you plan to find out about salary range and benefits:

_____ going to the public library and researching

_____ asking a friend who knows

_____ calling a nearby university and asking the Career Center

_____ going to an employment agency and asking for information

Questions You Might Ask the Interviewer

Some precise questions on your part show that you have studied the job, are intelligent, and seek a position to match your qualifications. You might consider these:

1. What qualities do you consider most important to success in this position?

2. What skills do you see as essential (if not listed on the job description)?

3. Who is the supervisor?

4. What kind of in-service training is expected? Is there a training plan?

5. How does this job fit into the (department, company, institutional) structure?
6. How is work evaluated? When? By whom?

WORKSHEET 62

Questions you will ask and why: _____

_____

a. _____

_____

b. _____

_____

c. _____

_____

d. _____

_____

Opening the Interview

Your maturity and social skills will help you to establish rapport. Greeting the receptionist, giving the interviewer a warm smile and a firm handshake, and using common courtesy will start you off naturally. Because interviews are conversations between two interested persons, no rigid rules can be applied. Being prepared, because you have practiced, and knowing that you are presenting your best self will make you confident and add to your success.

After the initial "talk about the weather," the core questions take center stage: why should we hire you and why do you want the job? Everything you say should assist in answering these key queries.

If directly asked, "Why should we hire you?" or "Why do you want this job?" your responses might be similar to the following statements. Remember, though, that generic answers need to be adapted to real life.

1. "I've studied your _____
                              (company, school, parish, etc.)
   and see that my experience _____ can
                                      (name one or two)
   transfer and help you."
2. "I'm impressed with your work with _____
   and want to be a part of helping _____."
3. "It is easy for me to handle several projects at a time, and I see that you need such a person to assist with _____.

Somewhere during the conversation, let your employer know that you do not just want a job or want to work, but that "I want to work for YOU!" Making it personal can help to make the difference.

WORKSHEET 63

How will you open the interview if given a chance?

_____

_____

_____

Closing the Interview

Take your cue from the interviewer and be ready to leave when he or she is. Having given your key data, you might want to sum up quickly your interest in the position. Asking what the next step will be or when you will hear about the decision is also appropriate. Thank the interviewer or the interviewing team, and the receptionist, and send a thank-you letter for the interview within forty-eight hours.

Do and Don't Tips

A few additional ideas you might ponder include the following:

DO

- arrive at least fifteen minutes early and know where to park the car (if needed).
- relax and let everyone know you "feel at home" because you want the job and do "feel at home."
- mentally rehearse what you will say.
- know, if possible, who the interviewer will be and who actually hires.
- know the job qualifications and how you meet them.
- know the company goals and philosophy.
- have a plan B if the position is filled.
- keep all comments job-related.
- accent personal qualities along with your skills.
- take time before answering a question.
- listen carefully and ask for clarification if necessary.
- sit forward, have friendly eye contact.

- answer in complete sentences and time the length of your answers by the interviewer's reaction.
- ask "Is that what you wanted to know?" or "Do you wish me to go on?"
- phrase questions in open-ended style rather than closed: "When do you hire?" and "What qualities do you seek?" rather than "Are you hiring now?" and "Do my qualities fit?"
- volunteer information: "I'd like to tell you why I believe your needs and my qualifications match"; "If you need (name two or three qualities or skills you possess), I have used them effectively in the past," and give concrete details quickly; or "I'd like to tell a short story that shows how I might meet your needs."
- be friendly with the secretary or receptionist.
- be alert and enthusiastic, but be "real."
- have references typed on 3 × 5 cards, ready if needed.
- use the company name.
- have pen and pencil handy.
- dress appropriately.
- use these "zingers" to emphasize your strengths:
    I can produce.
    I am a fast learner.
    I am cool under pressure.
    I can handle several projects at a time.
    I have high energy.
    I am loyal and hard-working.
    I enjoy doing.
    I am creative.

DON'T
- be late.
- rush in and sit down.

- fuss with hair, clothes, pens.
- give "Yes" and "No" answers.
- criticize former employers.
- talk politics, religion, or the like.
- interrupt.
- expect résumé to "say it all."
- give long speeches or preach.

WORKSHEET 64

1. Which ideas from the Do and Don't tips should *you* pay special attention to?

IMPORTANT TIP	WHY?
a. _____	_____
b. _____	_____
c. _____	_____

Practicing

After preparing your interview, practice what you will say and how. Go back to your self-assessment and line up your competencies, qualities, and values. Check your résumé and review your experience and background. Reread the job description and remember why you want the job. Don't get lost in the forest.

Choose some questions from page 207 and start pretending. While you jog, shower, dig in the garden, or vacuum the rug, TALK out your answers. Say them, shout them, but be sure to verbalize them. Tell why you want the job, why you are the best candidate, and what you will do to benefit your employer.

Relate your past experience, skills, and qualities; make yourself important and needed. Ask a friend to listen to and critique your ideas. Tape-record your practice and listen for your authenticity, enthusiasm, clarity, and control. Check your *uh*'s and *um*'s and listen to your voice quality. Have fun, role-play, and be the interviewee you dream about being.

But PRACTICE, PRACTICE, PRACTICE!

Visualize the employer, the room, how you look, the weather, the way you smile, and how you shake hands. Sit down and answer each question, one by one. Rehearse your successful interview as often as time permits. Be on center stage and "bring down the house"!

After the Interview

As soon as possible, take some time to debrief and reflect. While the experience is still fresh, jot down notes that will help at your next interview.

WORKSHEET 65

1. How did it go?

    GREAT   GOOD   SO-SO   FAIR

2. What was strong?

    _____your answers

    _____your overall manner

    _____your questions

    _____your knowledge of the job

    _____your listening

    _____

    _____

3. What questions might you have answered better?

   a. _____

   b. _____

   c. _____

4. What else would you change?

   a. _____

   b. _____

   c. _____

5. What did you learn for future reference?

   a. _____

   b. _____

   c. _____

CHAPTER 16

The Application Form

Some employers grant interviews from a résumé and cover letter. Others ask you to complete an application form, and some employers require all three.

If you have not completed an application form recently, you may be awed by the detailed information required.

Frequently you will complete the form in the personnel office or the employer's workplace. As you fill out the document, you may be observed for speed, personal mannerisms, and general appearance. So beware!

"Cheat Sheet"

Because the information asked for is detailed, carry index cards or take along a "Cheat Sheet" with pertinent facts:

- names, addresses, phone numbers of former employers

- dates of employment
- educational institutions
- degrees/years granted
- licenses or certifications, numbers, dates of expiration
- references, each with title, company, address, and phone number

Having this information ready eliminates asking to use the phone book or leaving blank spaces.

Other Tips

1. Take an extra pen or pencil. One applicant forgot this essential item and when he asked to borrow one, was refused. Another candidate obtained the job!

2. Consider your application form as a kind of introduction. It gives a quick preview of you as a person. It can also be stored away for future reference. Be careful, therefore, of what you say and how you say it. Paint an honest but attractive picture of yourself.

3. Only information related to the job may be requested—for example, the ability to lift, to type, to speak a second language. You are free to disregard inquiries not related to the job.

4. Never leave a blank space; it can indicate inattention, lack of preciseness, or carelessness. If the question does not apply, write "N.A." or mark a dash to indicate that you have read the question and it is not applicable.

5. Keep all data current and on your data "Cheat Sheet" (see Appendix, page 262) so your information is accessible at all times.

6. Make the application form a supportive element in your job-search packet; neat, carefully done, and complete, it reflects again your professional know-how.

7. Some job-seekers secure the application form ahead of time and type in all the information before presenting it. Think about that.

A Picture of You

From your job application alone, a potential employer can surmise:

1. *Who You Really Are:* A general picture of you can be drawn from the data you give. Characteristics revealing energy and initiative emerge. Your compatibility with the company can be measured. Some employers even utilize handwriting analysis to confirm their impressions.

2. *How Careful You Are:* Not following directions on a form could mean not following directions on the job, simple carelessness, or even poor reading skills.

3. *How You Work:* A neatly completed application can indicate one who cares about his or her work, who is efficient, and who carries through. An incomplete form can indicate someone who doesn't care about details or doesn't finish a task.

4. *Inner Drive:* A reviewer can surmise your personal motivation, determination, and creativity from the data you give about your experiences and education.

5. *Your Potential for Success:* By studying your jobs, volunteer work, leadership roles, and advancements, an employer can predict, to some extent, your performance in this new position.

6. *Your Stability:* Your work history may reveal your ability to relate to supervisors and coworkers; it may also reveal your stability (if you have held a job for many years), or lack of stability (if you have held many jobs for short periods of time). It may indicate your possible lack of flexibility (if you have held the same job for TOO many years).

Chapter 17

References

Some employers insist on references and some prefer to ignore them. Telephone calls often replace the written reference letter because calls can save time and legal entanglements. If you specifically need a letter of reference, request it; otherwise, simply ask the person who will affirm your qualifications if you may use his or her name and phone number for a possible reference call.

Even though these letters may be difficult to get, to keep up to date, and to fit the job you seek, they are important—so have them ready. Following are a few suggestions that might make the task a bit easier.

Whom to Ask

People who know you, know your work, and know your potential should be asked to write your references. A general rule to follow suggests having three references—two for your professional work and one for your character èndorsement. If you have no formal professional references, seek one from your pastor, rabbi, or minister, your doctor or other persons in the community who can confirm your value as a person and a potential employee. Never ask relatives for references.

How to Ask

Make writing your reference easy for a former employer, supervisor, or co-worker. Allow him or her at least two weeks to write the letter; supply all the information you think might be necessary:

- your legal name and address
- when you worked together
- tasks you (or both of you) did well
- qualities you have
- supporting data (successes reached, projects completed, or struggles overcome)
- your résumé and statement of your goals
- your recent activities and leadership positions

If you know the place of the interview and the person who will be interviewing you, have your reference-writer individualize the letter. Using his or her letterhead can add strength. If you do not have time for your reference to be personalized, have each letter addressed "To Whom It May Concern" or head it "Fine Qualifications of _____."

Some job-seekers keep their reference letters sealed and hand them to the interviewer when requested. Others have a file at a university placement office or employment agency for ready access.

3 × 5 Cards

Another practice is for job-seekers to have the name, address, and telephone number of each of their references on 3 × 5 cards ready to hand to an interviewer who asks. Be sure, however, if you do this to tell your references that you are looking for a job so they will be prepared for the important call from your prospective employer.

WORKSHEET 66

1. People you will ask for references are:

    a.   Name: _____

           Address: _____

           _____

           Phone: _____

    b.   Name: _____

           Address: _____

           _____

           Phone: _____

    c.   Name: _____

           Address: _____

           _____

           Phone: _____

2: Information you will give your reference-writers so they can easily write strong letters:
    a. Where you worked:

_____

_____

_____

b. What you did well:

1) _____

2) _____

3) _____

4) _____

c. Qualities you think you have:

1) _____

2) _____

3) _____

4) _____

d. Data that supports your qualifications and qualities:

1) _____

2) _____

3) _____

4) _____

Update your references each time you initiate a job search, and when you secure a job, be sure to thank those who wrote references for you. The thank-you letter, discussed in the next chapter, is another courtesy that fits your professional style!

CHAPTER 18

The Thank-You Letter

A thank-you letter expresses appreciation for any service given, and an interview—like a letter of reference—deserves such a touch of courtesy. Brief, sincere, professional, this letter is written to a specific person or group. Form letters are never appropriate.

What to Say and When

In writing your post-interview thank-you letter, just mention one or two top facts to keep you in the spotlight as decisions are made. You might repeat some key point that was discussed or some positive idea you want emphasized. But this is not the place to restate your application letter. Do, however, reiterate your interest in the position!

The letter should be written within forty-eight hours of the interview. This common courtesy reflects the fine candidate you are and frequently sets you apart from the crowd.

Even if you are not offered the job, your thank-you note

is often clipped to your application and résumé. And when an opening occurs at a later date, your courteous letter then stands out and highlights your qualifications and interest.

Type your letter and make it professional. See the next page for a sample letter showing how you can simply and sincerely say "Thank you."

Sample

Your Street Address
City, State   Zip
Date of Writing

Joan Warning, President
St. Henry's Pastoral Council
City, State   Zip

Dear Joan Warning:

Thank you for the time you spent last
Tuesday talking with me about your excellent
Volunteer Program for the Elderly at St.
Henry's Parish. I am impressed with your fine
organization and the involvement of so many
parishioners.

After speaking with you, I am sure that my
years of administration and my love for the
elderly will fit your needs. Ministering in a
parish such as yours would be both challenging
and a privilege.

Thank you for your warm welcome and gracious
hospitality. I hope that the pot-luck this
week was a success. I look forward to hearing
from you after the Council meets next Monday.

Sincerely,

Your Handwritten Name

Your Typed Name

Suggested Form

This is another generic letter, giving you a form you might use.

```
Your Present Address
City, State    Zip Code
Date of Writing

Name of Interviewer
Position or Title (if any)
Name of Organization
Address
City, State    Zip Code

Dear ____ :

1st Paragraph: Express thanks for the
interview, giving the place, date, and
position sought. Reinforce your interest in
the job: emphasize that you do want to work for
the organization, and tell why. (This can be
done in two or three SHORT sentences—do not be
profuse.)

2nd Paragraph: Highlight your skills,
abilities, and qualities related to the
position. Use this letter to remind the
interviewer of your chief strengths. (Again,
be direct and honest.) You may mention that
you will furnish further information if
needed.

3rd Paragraph: If fitting, indicate how
excited or eager you are at the prospect of
working with the organization or person; do
not say "anxious" as this denotes anxiety and
fear. Close cordially with a forward look.

Sincerely,

Your Handwritten Name

Your Typed Name
```

WORKSHEET 67

Items you will include in your thank-you letter are:

a. _____

_____

b. _____

_____

c. _____

_____

d. _____

_____

What Happens
After the
Decision? The
Cycle Continues

There is a season for everything, a time for every occupation under heaven: A time for giving birth, a time for dying; A time for planting, a time for uprooting what has been planted; A time for searching, a time for losing; A time for keeping, a time for throwing away

Ecclesiastes 3:1–3, 6

Being available to the Spirit means having continual sensitivity to the leadings—those nudges spoken of earlier—of grace in your daily life; not just in time of crisis or major transition, but all the time. The exhortation to "Pray always" really means that gentle in-touchness with a God who is real though hidden, reliable though subtle, a God who loves you to the very end and even farther.

Whether your journey through this book has brought you to a decision for change in your work or continuation where you are, the process has probably made you more conscious of the integration of work and prayer. It is that simple but profound "walking with God" that is the Christian's daily call in an active, even frenetic contemporary world.

Unquestionably you have been called to change. This does not of necessity mean to change your job or your career, but ultimately to change your way of presence to whatever your work is. Since discernment involves looking at possible alternatives, a prayerful, honest analysis of available options might bring you to a peaceful decision to remain where you are—thus speaks the Spirit for now! But that job or career, after your sincere and thoughtful work in the preceding sections of this book, will never be quite the same.

If your decision *has* been to move into a new career field, seek a new employer in your present field, or seek a redefinition of your job with your present employer, the same holds

true. Prayer does that. Things are never quite the same because *you* are never quite the same.

This section is about "what next." Yes, Virginia, there
really is a NEXT. God's call and the confirmation of that call
through life as it is—circumstances both within and outside
of personal control—are never finished. If a new job is accepted, you pick up and begin anew to attend to the Spirit's
call to fullness of life in Christ through daily work. If no job
shift is chosen, you begin anew to attend to the situations,
the challenges, the opportunities already at hand, confident
that you are not alone in your daily routine.

Wherever your prayer and your best efforts to know and
do God's will may take you, peace goes with you when your
faith and your future are one.

CHAPTER 19

Accepting a New Job

S o you've explored the field, set your target, made your successful bid, and received the big phone call that the job is yours—if you want it.

"If I want it!" you might say. "You're kidding! Why would I have sweated through this whole process if I didn't want it?"

Relax! Recognize once again the gracious courtesy of God who often gives you the opportunity to think about a change, check it out, explore the possibilities.

Most job offers include an acceptance or negotiation interview. The circumstances are different from those of the job-candidacy interview; anxiety is down to a more normal level, blood pressure along with it. Still, unknowns are present and a new sense of anticipation sparks you to look your best, be prepared, and put both best feet—newly confirmed in the employer's grace—forward. By the way, congratulations!

Finalizing Details

If you have already decided that this is the job you want, the big phone call can be the vehicle for setting up an appointment to finalize details before beginning your work. This is a prudent step, even though you may feel you know all the answers. Worksheet #68 offers a list of items you may need to check on before you are officially on the payroll.

If any of these are not clear to you when the job is offered, both you and the employer will benefit by confirming them before day one. An acceptable compromise might be "This will be explained at our new-employee seminar on Friday," or "This copy of our handbook covers many of your fine questions. I'll clarify anything still at issue after you've had a chance to study it."

WORKSHEET 68

1. Points you may wish to clarify at an acceptance or negotiation interview:

    a. work hours, check-in and -out procedures, lunch and break policies

    b. compensation, benefits

    c. work area, supplies, equipment available to you

    d. training opportunities, requirements, support

    e. growth-assessment procedures, evaluations

    f. supervisory responsibilities, limitations

    g. line of authority; who reports to whom and in what manner

    h. dress code, behavior code (e.g., smoking issues)

    i. personal convenience (e.g., parking, locker space, exercise areas)

     j.   whom to refer to as questions arise; orientation pro-
         cedures

2.   Add other questions or points for clarification:

_____

_____

_____

_____

The Confirmation Letter

If a job offer is made by letter, it is appropriate to respond by letter, reviewing your basic understanding of the job offer and the terms of employment. If you and the prospective employer are not in agreement, this allows for clarification before a final commitment is made. The confirmation letter is especially important when a long-distance job change is in question. Be sure to clarify the company's moving policies, and its relocation agents or moving firms if any. Include in the letter your appreciation for the employer's confidence in you and for all courtesies extended during the application/interview process.

A sample acceptance letter is found in the Appendix on page 268. Follow any similar content, use a professional format, and make it sincere and straightforward.

Mopping-Up Operations

When a new job has been accepted, formalities and courtesies relating to transition are in order. Consider the following in terms of their relevance to your situation:

1. *Giving notice to current employer:* Leaving a job as graciously and considerately as possible is not only professional behavior but also Christian courtesy. Know your current employer's policy on notice; two weeks is the usual. Be prepared to offer support and appropriate help in covering your position while replacement is being arranged. Even in situations in which relations have been strained between you and an employer (or co-workers), your ability to go the extra mile in helping with an easy transition will redound to your credit and demonstrate your good will.

    Important: be sure the current employer's needs and policies regarding resignation are made known to and negotiated with the new employer. Your sensitivity and loyalty will highlight your reliability and affirm the choice the new employer has made.

2. *Withdrawing from other candidacies:* Once a new job is accepted, or when a decision is made not to change jobs, advise others who have you in serious consideration that you are no longer available. This can be done with a courteous, brief letter. Include your appreciation for the employer's consideration, your respect for the company, and your best wishes for their success in finding the right person for the opening. A sample withdrawal note is offered on page 269 in the Appendix.

3. *Recognizing the support of others:* Sit down and make a list of those who have been your special support during your time of search. This might include relatives, friends, professional colleagues, your pastor, counselors, and/or teachers. A note or a phone call announcing the good news, and expressing your thanks for help given, will underscore the confidence these people have had in you, and create a bond of friendship that can pay dividends over the years. A later note letting them know how it is working out

for you would also be a gesture they will remember warmly. (See Appendix, page 272.)

4. *Letting others know of your new situation:* Many individuals find it valuable to make a simple announcement of their new work location to those who might be affected by the change. This is especially important for persons in people-serving work: health care, personal services, any profession or trade in which an individual has worked person-to-person and has something of a "clientele." It can also be a gracious gesture to colleagues, and other persons in the same field, with whom contacts will be maintained. And certainly it recognizes the interest, and values the good wishes, of those who encourage your career development. Such an announcement can also correct mailing lists for publications you receive at work and wish to continue receiving at your new job site.

WORKSHEET 69

Great! You've accepted the new job! With whom do you want to share the news?

1. Those who have supported and/or helped with the job search:

Name	Special thanks for:	Call	Write
a.			
b.			
c.			
d.			
e.			
f.			
g.			

h. _____

i. _____

j. _____

2. Clients/Colleagues who would be interested in your
    new position:

    Name   Call   Send Announcement

    a. _____

    b. _____

    c. _____

    d. _____

    e. _____

    f. _____

    g. _____

    h. _____

    i. _____

    j. _____

5. *Celebrating:* Do! The completion of a job search is
    cause for celebration. Perhaps going out for pizza
    with your best friend would do it. Or maybe it will
    be a special family dinner, a long-distance call home
    to share the good news, or—if it's *that* kind of job—
    a Caribbean cruise! You decide. Just be sure to punc-
    tuate a new beginning with joy, gratitude, and a treat
    for yourself.

CHAPTER 20

Staying Where You Are

hat if your prayerful, practical review of your work situation suggests that it is best to remain where you are?

First of all, this is a valid, honorable decision. No two sets of circumstances are the same in human life. Only *you* can make the final decision. With trust in a God who loves and cares for you, and with the prudent counsel of others who also love and care, you may decide that where you are is the holiest place in the world. For you. At this time. Even if it has warts!

In six months, a year, three years, something may change and you will begin again prayerfully to explore the job possibilities. Be ready and willing for this. In the meantime, what you have is precious—because you and God have agreed it is right for you now. Resolve that each day on the job will open new avenues. Determine to make the most of your situation, with faith in your future; be confident that your present job has great potential. Consider the points discussed in the following sections of this chapter.

Learning, Training, Self-Improvement

Evaluate your work situation for its potential. Ask yourself whether, while working there, you can increase any skills you found weak in your personal assessment, talents you know are there but have never been developed. Check out company-provided training; apply for workshops, seminars, in-service opportunities. Also look outside the work situation; explore short courses, special programs, conferences, regular classes offered by local colleges and universities. Investigate correspondence courses, church adult education offerings, community schools, local park and recreation department programs. What's out there for YOU? Not only can you build your skills, develop your talents, gain confidence for career development—you can also expand your attitudes and develop new insights into the dynamics of your job and the rest of your life as well.

This approach is particularly significant if you feel that your decision to remain in your present job is dictated largely by circumstances rather than by your 'druthers and/or God's call; that is, if you feel it's "the way things are for now." Moping never got anyone anywhere. Use your time wisely, with faith in a future that you know will be available to you eventually. Such an attitude will help to make that future a here-and-now experience.

WORKSHEET 70

1. Since you're continuing in your present job for now, what self-development issues do you want to attack? List

the skills you'd like to improve in the next twelve months:

a. _____

b. _____

c. _____

d. _____

e. _____

2. Now rank these in the order of their value to you at this time:

Most important: _____

Would be valuable: _____

Helpful, not essential: _____

Could be helpful: _____

Just for fun: _____

3. Determine what resources are available to help you develop one or more of these target skills. If you find no accessible resources to help you with your "most important" choice, don't back down! Move on to other skills, even to the one that's "just for fun." Look into:

company-sponsored training

college credit courses

non-credit courses

workshops, seminars

individual tutoring

personal reading, study

YM/YWCAs

kits, workbooks, videos

correspondence courses

volunteer work

public library/museum programs

park and recreation dept. services

professional and trade associations

medical center programs

computer centers   local agencies

public-school-district
 "community school"
 services

Seeking the Best

There is scarcely a work situation imaginable—well, maybe the Bob Cratchit-Ebenezer Scrooge arrangement is an exception—where there aren't some lights at the end of the various tunnels of the weekly routine. Seek them out. You may have to be an initiator, courageous in trying a new idea, demonstrating consideration and thoughtfulness, refusing to be part of the office conspiracy, keeping your mouth shut sometimes and opening it at others.

If a work situation is genuinely dehumanizing, demoralizing, or just plain awful, others feel it, too. You may find people like yourself seeking to make the day's work more productive, the workplace happier and less stressful. Risk giving these co-workers cause for hope by your own determination and follow-through. If you seek Christ in the marketplace, you will find Him. And though it took some powerful nightmares to bring about Scrooge's renewal, Bob was the happiest man on earth to be there when it happened.

WORKSHEET 71

1. List those co-workers you feel have a genuinely positive influence in your workplace, by their attitudes and/or actions.

    a. _____

    b. _____

    c. _____

Tell at least one of these people why you put him or her on this list.

2. List three situations at work in which you have the ability to act with integrity and a positive spirit regardless of what others choose, or appear to choose, to do:

    a. _____

    b. _____

    c. _____

Circle the one you'll commit yourself to first.

3. List three ways in which you could brighten, enliven, beautify, cheer, or otherwise improve your place of work:

    a. _____

    b. _____

    c. _____

Do at least one of these by this time next week.

4. Try doing this exercise once a month—perhaps even once a week. Watch yourself take off!

Concentrating on Quality

Focusing on superb performance or a superior product can revitalize you and minimize the gnats and mosquitoes swarming around your daily work situation. You may already be performing wonderfully or crafting exquisite products; that's fine—rejoice and be glad! Enjoy the quality of your work: admire the beautifully prepared proposal, savor the richness of your "chef's special" sauce, enjoy the "purr" of the engine you've just tuned. Open the doors of your consciousness to the powers that bless the results of your work. Avoid dwelling on the flaws and fumbles. Know them only as things that your giftedness can polish and transform, making them into products and performances that will continue to be beautiful praises to God, who is beautiful first.

Sure, it's nice to be appreciated, to have your work recognized for its quality. But the one who must ultimately appreciate and recognize it is yourself. Keep your eyes on the quality of your work, accept your own satisfaction in what you know is good about it, and less energy will go into difficult workaday details.

WORKSHEET 72

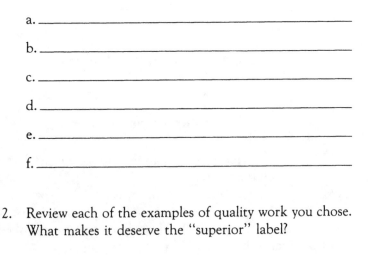

1. What pieces of work in the past six months do you look back on with most pride? (Reports written, engines renewed, quotas reached, jobs completed, sales made, deals closed, clients served, problems solved . . .)

    a. _____

    b. _____

    c. _____

    d. _____

    e. _____

    f. _____

2. Review each of the examples of quality work you chose. What makes it deserve the "superior" label?

    a. _____

    b. _____

c. _____

d. _____

e. _____

f. _____

Do you find any patterns in the characteristics of your quality work? Keep watching, savoring those characteristics in the work you produce during this coming month—and every month thereafter. Congratulations!

Listening to the Spirit

Setting aside a few minutes of quiet reflection at the end of each workday may be the most productive thing you do. It can be while you're still at your desk, in the car going home, or on the street during the few minutes' walk from the bus stop to the front door.

Use a simple prayer formula: "Dear Lord, I worked for You today. Show me where You were in the day we spent together." Then allow God to do what you've asked. Let the day at work swing past you: The opportunities to grow you've accepted and rejected. The small gifts—a word of praise from a co-worker, a contract finalized, that hoped-for phone call coming through. Kindnesses given and received. Anxieties shared. A really rough staff meeting that left you angry and defensive. Anne confiding that Steve had lost his job and how afraid they are, with the baby coming. Allow the words, the faces, the symbols to surface as God links them together with the insights of previous days and years. Accept the growing awareness of the Lord's presence in the persons, events, things that make up your day. Thank God for being there with you. Remind your Creator of how glad you are for continued faithfulness each tomorrow.

This simple five-minute daily habit may make the work world a very different place for you as the months roll on, and can make "staying where you are" the most remarkable of experiences.

CHAPTER 21

Continuing the
Exploration

Regardless of whether you move into a new job or remain in your present one, the daily task of attending to the voice of the Spirit remains constant.

That new job is an important career step, a milestone in your history, perhaps the crown of a long journey from apprenticeship to mastery of your trade. The old job, with its relationships to the other dimensions of your life, may also be all those things, viewed from a different mountaintop. Wherever you work, the Lord works with you, inviting you deeper into the mystery of God's love for the world and for you in particular. Whatever decision you make after prayer, thought, counsel, study, and reflection, these ongoing tasks once again face you; they are never finished "once and for all."

1. *You are called* to learn how your gifts, skills, and the sum of your experiences match the needs in this given situation for the maturing of God's Kingdom.

It stands to reason, then, that you are called continually to recognize, accept, and foster your talents, and to develop through practice the skills your talents generate.

2. *You are called* to be sensitive and attentive to the dynamics of your given situation so that the Spirit who is present within it will be known and loved. The stresses of each day's schedule, of human relationships, and of personal ambivalence are the language of grace; learn to listen in moments—brief or extended—of solitude.

3. *You are called* to constant renewal of values and attitudes, measures of the quality of your work and of your life. Renewal asks that you articulate these measures of quality, not only to God in prayer but also to whatever human community you claim as your own. As a human being you are designed to support, assist, cherish other persons. The purpose of work is to enable the human community to survive and prosper. That community, informed by the Spirit, can keep you honest, steadfastly renewing you as you trust it and share with it the best and the worst of yourself.

4. *You are called* to maintain a healthy life balance that puts work and play on a par. That recognizes all the facets of human living as good, and worthy of respect. Reasonable care for yourself provides a foundation for performance, productivity, and all that future you have so much faith in. Martyrdom is not an acceptable option until your work for the Kingdom is ready for crowning, not a moment before!

Whatever your next step is in the business of earning a living, plan your cycle of attention/ prayer, analysis/ prayer, decision/ prayer, action/ prayer, evaluation/ prayer, and attention. Be at peace with its spiral; it does lead somewhere. As T. S. Eliot once wrote:

> We shall not cease from exploration
> And the end of all our exploring
> Will be to arrive where we started
> And to know the place for the first time.

Appendix

CALENDAR PLANNING GUIDE: Duplicate this page and make yourself monthly "job-search calendars." Use to record résumés submitted, networking contacts made, interviews scheduled, whatever needs tracking along the way. Don't forget to include some scheduled treats for yourself. The laborer is worthy of his and her hire!

Month of _____ , 19 _____

Monday	Tuesday	Wednesday	Thursday	Friday	Saturday	Sunday

Goals/targets for this month: _____

_____

End-of-the-month review: _____

_____

POWER VERBS   Use these action words on your résumé,
cover letter, and whenever you wish to accent positively your
experiences.

achieved	devised	installed
acquired		instructed
administered	earned	integrated
advanced	educated	invented
advised	effected	
analyzed	employed	led
appeased	established	lent
applied	evaluated	located
arbitrated	executed	
arranged	expanded	maintained
assisted	extended	managed
assumed		marketed
	facilitated	mastered
built	fashioned	monitored
	focused	motivated
clarified	formed	
completed	founded	negotiated
composed		netted
conceived	generated	
conducted	governed	obtained
consulted	guided	operated
controlled		organized
converted	handled	
coordinated	headed	participated
created		passed
	implemented	perfected
demonstrated	improved	performed
designed	increased	piloted
determined	influenced	pioneered
developed	initiated	planned

procured
produced
promoted
proposed
proved
provided

reconciled
reduced
related
regulated
reorganized

replaced
reported
researched
reworked

secured
served
settled
simplified
sold
solved

strengthened
structured
succeeded

taught
trained
transferred
transformed

unified
united

DATA SHEET (As discussed in Chapter 21)   Basic information for use on résumés and applications. Keep up-to-date for *quick reference* at any time!

Social Security # _____

Licenses/Certifications

(Numbers/dates): _____

Birthdate: _____

Birthplace: _____

References: (Note: ask permission before giving someone's name as a reference)

Name	Address

Special skills, competencies, interests, hobbies:

_____

_____

_____

Publications, exhibits, special projects (note date, place, if applicable):

_____

_____

_____

_____

_____

Telephone   Comments

Professional/Work Experience:

Job Title	Employer	Location/Address

Education/Professional Preparation:

School	Location	Dates: From/To

Dates: From/To	Salary	Supervisor

Degree/Cert.	Major/Minor/Course/Program

Awards/Honors:

Identification   Awarded by

_____

_____

_____

_____

_____

Volunteer/Community Service:

Service   Location/Agency/Etc.

_____

_____

_____

_____

_____

Memberships/Participation:

Organization   Nature of Participation

_____

_____

_____

_____

_____

Date	Recognition for

Title (if any)	From/To	Significant Facts

From/To	Leadership	From/To

A Accepting A Job

written acceptance note is binding, so be sure you want the job. Then write to confirm your decision. It is wise to confirm important details negotiated verbally at the final interview; for example, salary and benefits, starting date, moving allowance. Most large businesses provide these items in writing, but if you do not have such an agreement, it is best to verify the details when accepting the job. If all aspects have been taken care of, just write a friendly, professional letter.

```
Your Street Address
City, State  Zip
Date of Writing

Name of Employer, Title if Appropriate
Name of Company
Address

Dear _____:
```

I am pleased to accept the coordinator position in your service department. The terms we discussed are satisfactory, and I have enclosed my signed agreement.

The health forms should reach you within the week as I have asked to have them sent directly to your office.

As agreed, I will be ready to start on Monday, October 10. Thank you again for your time and consideration. I look forward to working with you at _____.

```
Sincerely,

Your Handwritten Name

Your Typed Name
```

Declining a Job Offer

When declining a job, give the reasons, if possible. Time and consideration have been given to you as an applicant, so reciprocate with the same professional courtesy.

```
Your Street Address
City, State Zip
Date of Writing

Name of Possible Employer, Title if Appropri-
ate
Name of Company
Address

Dear _____:

    Your position of _____ truly interests
me, and I am pleased with your offer to work
at _____. Your program looks exciting and
offers a fine opportunity.

    As we discussed, however, my experience and
interest lie in working in rural areas, and
another group has offered me a job in its
Outreach program. Because my wish to work with
rural families can be readily met by the other
program, I have accepted the job offer.

    Thank you for your consideration and
kindness. I appreciate the hour you spent
talking with me and hope your program
continues to grow.

Sincerely,

Your Handwritten Name

Your Typed Name
```

Requesting An Earlier Decision

I f a job offer involves a conflict of time, you may wish to ask for a change of deadlines. The following letter faces the facts simply and clearly.

```
Your Street Address
City, State Zip
Date of Writing

Name of Employer, Title if Appropriate
Name of Company
Address

Dear _____:

   When we talked about the coordinator posi-
tion at the Food Bank, last week, you said you
would let me know your decision before April
1. Although your position is still my first
choice and I hope to accept it, another parish
has offered me a position and asks that I let
them know within the next ten days.

   Because I wish to work at a Food Bank, and
because your program seems to offer a greater
service and to fit my experience, I would
appreciate knowing your decision before
Tuesday, March 29.

   If you need more information, please let me
know. I can be reached weekdays between 8:00
A.M. and 5:00 P.M. at 326-3436, and in the eve-
nings at 328-4220.

   Thank you for considering this request. I
look forward to hearing from you.

Sincerely,

Your Handwritten Name

Your Typed Name
```

Requesting An Extension

If you need an extension of time before accepting a job, and have legitimate reasons, a request may be made. A risk is entailed but your reasons can prove your sincerity.

```
Your Address
City, State Zip
Date of Writing

Name of Employer, Title if Appropriate
Name of Company
Address

Dear _____:
```

The coordinator position you offered me in your May 3 letter is an exciting challenge and opportunity. Thank you for your confidence in me.

Because of a death in my family, I would appreciate your giving me until May 15 to make a decision. Family obligations may affect my employment plans.

Your program impresses me and is my first choice. If you can allow me the extra days, I would be most grateful.

Thank you for considering my request.

Sincerely,

Your Handwritten Name

Your Typed Name

W Thanking Those Who Helped

rite a note to thank those who supported you by writing references or assisting in your successful job search. It's nice to be remembered for helping.

```
Your Address
City, State Zip
Date of Writing
Dear _____.

   Your support during my recent job search has
been greatly appreciated. I'm happy to tell
you that I have accepted a position with _____
and will begin _____.

   Thank you for your reference, suggesting
contacts or openings, being there when I
needed to talk or whatever the assistance
was. I hope to be able to support others in
their job searches as generously as you have
supported me.

Sincerely,

Your Name
```

This letter can be more formal if the one you are thanking is not a personal friend. Adjust your letter to fit the situation.

THE JOB TRAIL

POSITION	WITH (Company)	RESUME SENT TO	ON (Date)	FOLLOW-UP CONTACT (Date)	Comment	INTERVIEW (Date)	Comment	TY (Thank You) sent	IMPRESSIONS

Printed in the United States
by Baker & Taylor Publisher Services